COLLISION OVER
VIETNAM

COLLISION OVER VIETNAM

A FIGHTER PILOT'S STORY OF SURVIVING
THE ARC LIGHT ONE TRAGEDY

DON HARTEN

TURNER

Turner Publishing Company

200 4th Avenue North • Suite 950
Nashville, TN 37219

445 Park Avenue • 9th Floor
New York, NY 10022

www.turnerpublishing.com

Collision Over Vietnam:
A Fighter Pilot's Story of Surviving the Arc Light One Tragedy

A previous edition of this book was published under the title
Arc Light One. Views and opinions expressed are not necessarily those of the Department of Defense or Department of the Air Force.

Cover design by Mike Penticost

Library of Congress Cataloging-in-Publication Data

Harten, Don.
 Collision over vietnam : a fighter pilot's story of surviving the Arc Light One tragedy /
Don Harten.
    p. cm.
"A previous edition of this book was published under the title Arc Light One"--T.p.
verso.
 ISBN 978-1-59652-836-9
1.   Vietnam War, 1961-1975--Aerial operations, American. 2.   Vietnam War,
1961-1975--Personal narratives, American. 3.   Harten, Don. I. Harten, Don. Arc Light
One. II. Title.
 DS558.8.H385 2011
 959.704'348092--dc23
 [B]

                                                                2011029963

Printed in the United States of America
11 12 13 14 15 16 17 — 0 9 8 7 6 5 4 3 2 1

This book is dedicated to the families of the men who
were killed in the midair collision during
ARC LIGHT ONE

James M. Gehrig, Jr.
Tyrell G. Lowry
William E. Neville
Joe C. Robertson
James A. Marshall
Robert L. Armond
Frank P. Watson
Harold J. Roberts, Jr.

Contents

Acknowledgments

Few people write anything worthwhile all by themselves. Why? Writers cannot see the forest for all the trees. We see the details and must rely upon others to point out where we might wander from the path. I profoundly thank my dear friend, Carole Thompson, editor of the MiG Sweep, for proofing the book and for insisting that I follow correct paths through the forest of words. I also thank my mother, Lucille Harten, a brilliant woman, for insisting upon correcting my penchant for splitting infinitives. So, to really get her attention, I constructed a five-word split infinitive and hid it somewhere. Now neither of us can find it! Thanks also to Mary Harnes for helping me with the photographs. If anyone ever finds the five-word split infinitive, please let my mother know. I don't really care! (See!)

Preface

It took nearly forty years to write this book. My mind buried it deeper as each year passed until I wondered if I'd ever remember anything. Yet, when I forced the events of a head-on, midair collision of two B-52's to the surface of my mind, they were as vivid as the night they occurred. Although I could talk about it with close friends or family occasionally, I could not write about it. So I procrastinated. Besides, it seems nobody wanted anything to do with the Vietnam War and its remembrance. September 11, 2001, made it relevant once again.

Until my dying day I will maintain that the first combat mission ever flown by the Strategic Air Command, ARC LIGHT ONE, would have stopped the Vietnam War cold in its tracks before it even got started. Instead, our political leaders tried to play at toy soldiers when they knew nothing about combat, war, or the military. The result was millions dying during and after our involvement. This one mission would have eliminated communist aggression in one day with 30 B-52's. Instead, it took eight years, millions of lives, and 130 B-52's twelve days during the Christmas bombings of 1972.

I realized, finally, that this story could only be told in first person intimate. I had to place the reader behind my eyes and into my head in order to let him see and really feel what happened. Every word is as accurate as I can remember it. Literary license was used only once, in a minor time shift for continuity. Every conversation in dialogue took place, although I could not remember each word exactly. That being said, during the crash sequence every word spoken is exactly what was said at the time, as those moments are still burned into my mind. I did soften one profanity uttered just prior to the midair collision.

Chapter Three, which is an overview of the Cold War leading up to Vietnam, was thoroughly researched and every fact in the chapter was multiply verified. Of course, some tried to modify history—and they succeeded somewhat in the minds of many people—but few revisionists ever were in Vietnam! I was there, literally from the opening shot of the war until the very end. I flew another tour in B-52's, later an extended tour in F-105's, and yet another in F-111's during the Linebacker Operations that ended the war. We won and later gave it away politically! Result: the Killing Fields.

COLLISION OVER
VIETNAM

Chapter One

The silver tails of eight B-52F bombers stood like a group of tall buildings above the gently sloping rise beside the runway. The bombers squatted in silence, their wings drooping like huge birds of prey guarding their eggs and waiting—waiting for nuclear war. Each bomber held several times more firepower than had ever been expended by all participants in all the wars in the history of the planet. Hundreds of B-52's were built for the sole purpose of delivering thermonuclear weapons to any despot foolish enough to attempt an attack upon America—and thus, the world lived in an uneasy peace throughout a Cold War that often got hot.

The low angle of early morning sunshine reflected off one of the huge tails, illuminating the grass and a profusion of yellow field flowers at my feet. The air was fresh and the wind gentle against my cheek. That summer of 1964, I felt immensely proud to finally wear Air Force pilot wings. My active flying career in the Strategic Air Command would begin in just a few minutes. Savoring the moment, I stretched myself tall and popped my finest salute toward the eight B-52's sitting quietly on nuclear alert. The bombers were asleep and didn't see my salute, but that was okay because soon we would get to know each other—how well would, in time, amaze me.

The screech of idling jet engines drowned out the sounds of the morning as another of the giants taxied toward the runway to fly a training mission. Both its size and the noise it produced dominated the scene. I waved to the pilot as the B-52 rolled past me and he waved back. I didn't know him but at that moment I felt a kinship with him, a feeling of belonging to something very special. I climbed down into my red MGA sports car to hurry to the end of the runway for an up-close view of the behemoth taking off.

A large sign beside the ring road said, "ALERT CREW QUICK ACCESS ROAD." This was the path to my future, the alert pad, where I had been instructed to go for my first day of Strategic Air Command (SAC) training. I turned up the road and stopped just short of the end of the runway, got out and waved again to the B-52 pilot as he taxied onto the runway for takeoff. This time he didn't wave back to me, but rather he pointed toward his left wing tip. I wondered about that and thought he might be checking something on his plane. I would soon learn why he signaled me that way, simply one more of a myriad of lessons to be learned in order to understand the Strategic Air Command.

The B-52 angled onto the runway, its engines screeching higher and higher, the noise becoming deafening. I held my ears as the pilot brought the engines to full power. The exhaust roiled back toward me until I could feel the heat from the eight jets when, inexplicably, the noise from them diminished to silence. For a moment I couldn't figure out what had happened until I realized the power from those engines so churned the air directly behind them that all the sound waves were broken up and swallowed in the turbulence. Soon though, the jet roar returned.

I watched the B-52 roll down the runway, slowly gaining speed and belching a black smoke trail from the water injection. It lifted off the runway, sort of tail first in the manner of loaded B-52's, and roared into the sky in a very slow climb. When it turned left, climbing away from the city of Sacramento, I turned back to reality, got into my MG again, and headed for the alert pad with childlike dreams of flying on my mind.

Like a medieval castle, the nuclear alert facility, known as the "alert pad," dominated the rise beside the runway. It was a prime nuclear target, ground zero for Soviet missiles. Inside the pad, aircrews and maintenance teams lived in relative comfort during their alert tours. The bottom floor of the pad, buried in an earthen berm, was the sleeping quarters for the alert crews. The upper floor contained a full mess hall, a large, modern briefing room, a small library, a game room with both pool and Ping-Pong tables, a television room, numerous aircrew study rooms, and a command center.

Long sloping ramps led from both levels of the alert pad to the "Christmas tree," where the B-52's, sitting nuclear alert, waited for war. The Christmas tree was a massive concrete taxiway with ten hardstands, each the size of a city block, that angled into the trunk of the tree. From there the tree's trunk flowed down the rise and onto the runway at an angle, which was designed for a rolling getaway in case the bad guys raised the battle flag.

On the base side of the Christmas tree was a small guard shack where I stopped my MG and said a nice "good morning" to one of the two guards. I fully expected a sharp salute from him even though I wore only the gold bars of a second lieutenant. Instead of saluting, the bastard pointed his rifle at me!

"GET OUT! GET OUT!" he shouted. "Hands above your head! Put your face on the ground!" He yelled these things at me. Hey, wait! I'm an officer and you're not supposed to talk to me like that. Now, how the hell am I supposed to keep my hands above my head and put my face on the ground while trying to get out of my MG?

Suddenly, I knew the answer. Another guard poked his rifle at me through the other window. I wanted to yell back at both of them but they had guns pointed right at my face.

"Okay, okay," I said. I kept my hands up and the first

guard carefully opened my car door, and then stepped back. I knew that if I moved quickly the second guard would shoot and later they would fill out forms.

I slowly climbed out of the car without using my hands, which were well away from my center of balance, and then I kind of kneeled and fell to one elbow, then to fully prone. The guard pushed the end of his rifle barrel into my neck and told me not to move. Right, like I had the ability to do anything but quiver. I was frozen to the warm concrete.

Almost immediately a whole truckload of security police were upon me. A technical sergeant told me to stand up and keep my hands locked to the top of my head. I did as he directed.

"May I speak?" I asked hesitantly. Three guards that I could see kept their rifles pointed at my head, my chest, and my genitals. I was certain there was another guard or two behind me and just as certain that none of them would hesitate to shoot if I so much as moved an eyelid.

"No!" the tech sergeant said.

So I stood there feeling quite foolish, unable to do or say anything in explanation. Within seconds another truckload of security police arrived and by now there were about a dozen guards pointing guns at me while their sergeants talked excitedly on "bricks," small walkie-talkies. The tech sergeant put his nose close to my face and stared through my sunglasses directly into my eyes. He backed off a bit, looked me up and down, and finally said, "Okay, Lieutenant, get into the rear of that truck. And do it carefully."

I did as I was told and found three more unsmiling guards sitting in the back of the truck pointing their rifles at me. There was no way I could tell them this was all a big mistake, that they could at least smile. I was certain they were all laughing inside, reinforcing the old battle between enlisted man and officer as to which group was stupider. There was no doubt in their minds. We drove for about ten minutes and stopped alongside a remote building away from the main part of the air base.

"Get out, Lieutenant! Do it slow!" It was the voice of the same tech sergeant. I did as he ordered. "Face up against that wall, stand about three feet back, spread your legs, and place your hands on the wall." I did as he ordered, certain that he was enjoying all this. My entire visual field was the green shake wall where I stared at an exposed nail for twenty more minutes. I was acutely aware of the guards behind me and became increasingly convinced they would probably shoot me in the back of the head and dump my body somewhere. My arms ached. This was not "fun and games" training, these guys were as serious as a heart attack.

That damned nail was beginning to get obnoxious by the time I heard a friendly voice say, "It's okay, Sarge, he's one of our new guys." Then I felt a gentle tap on my shoulder as the same voice said, "You can relax now, Lieutenant."

I turned to see a master sergeant who was wearing a silly grin. His name tag indicated his last name was Savely and his smile told me he had dealt with second lieutenants before.

"You okay?" he asked.

"Yeah, but my arms ache."

"Sorry, Sir."

He said "sir" to me—now we were getting somewhere.

"We thought you knew where the main gate to the alert pad was. It's on the other side of the Christmas tree. This is the quick access road and it's for alert response vehicles only."

"Now you tell me," I said. So, that was why the B-52 pilot was pointing toward his left wing. I was wilted in the heat of the morning sun. Hot, sweaty, and completely embarrassed, I was going to meet my new squadron looking downright unmilitary and feeling like a jerk. My introduction to the Strategic Air Command was certainly ignominious.

Within a couple of months I had recovered some dignity and became just another aircrew member who spent about half his life, day and night, on the alert pad. As the new copilot on Crew E-06, the rest of my aircrew felt it was their duty to break me in. Basically, I became the "gofer" and they would have called me that except the accepted practice was to call me "Copilot."

SAC bomber crews were an integral unit. We flew together, of course, and served on alert together. With regular duty days, flight planning, briefings, and such, we spent very little time away from each other. Therefore, in SAC's infinite wisdom, the aircrew unit was reinforced.

Bomber crews have always had a crew order separate

from military rank. B-52 aircrews lined up in this order: pilot, copilot, radar navigator, navigator, electronic warfare officer, and gunner. Just like in the movies, we sat in briefings and lined up for things according to crew order. In the air we talked over the interphone, addressing each other by position such as, "Pilot, Nav, turn left to one niner seven." "Roger, Nav, left, one nine seven."

On the ground, even socially, everyone called each other by his crew position, almost never by his name and definitely NOT by his military rank unless it was for a military offense. When we talked "about" somebody, well, then it was okay to use his rank. We usually had eight aircrews on alert— that's forty-eight guys using this terminology—and it could have been confusing but we grew so close that we knew each other's voices even in a room full of chatter. It was almost intimate, like when we were kids at a family gathering and an aunt said to do something. We ignored the voice until Mom said, "Do it!" That voice we knew. Often we'd hear things like, "Hey Radar, where's the Copilot? The AC and Gunner want to go play handball." And Radar would respond, "Oh, he's with the Nav and EW doing mission study."

We called our Aircraft Commander "AC" on the ground and "Pilot" in the air. Otherwise, he was Major Jim Gehrig, a big man, gentle for his size and gentle on the stick in the air. He was from Pennsylvania and was not baseball great Lou Gehrig's cousin like I wanted to believe. But he was the first pilot in SAC to become a B-47 aircraft commander as a first lieutenant.

Our radar navigator was Major Bill Hart, one of those pleasant guys who was genuinely nice. Bill always had a smile or a joke ready to ease the natural tension that became life in SAC. His favorite saying was, "That's close enough for government work," usually referring to nuclear bomb deliveries since the radar navigator was the bombardier. His second favorite saying was, "Nothing is too good for SAC's combat crews—and that's exactly what they're going to get, nothing!" Sometimes he added, "And that's too good for them."

Captain Terry Lowry was possibly the best navigator in SAC and certainly one of the best I ever flew with. He thought like Radar O'Reilly on M*A*S*H and usually had answers for us before we finished our questions. Terry was quirky, intelligent, and fun to be around. We called him Nav as in, "Hey Nav, how much longer . . . " "Seven minutes!" " . . . grr . . . 'til . . . the next . . . ? Hmm, okay, thanks."

Jim Erbes was our electronic wizard, a first lieutenant who outranked me by about a year. It was only important to me because I had to be the gofer until a new second lieutenant joined the crew. Erbes was a quiet guy, very considerate, hard-working, and smart. Electronic Warfare Officers (EWO's) are probably the smartest guys in the Air Force, if not the whole world, and they are selected for that very reason. They are so smart that some of them are considered weird by us normal people. We called Jim "EW" for short. He could sleep anywhere, anytime as nothing fazed him.

And then God made gunners—a different breed. Quite young for a master sergeant, Bill Neville was our gunner. He was probably the most street-smart man I ever knew and he was good looking by any standards, painfully so for the rest of us. Whenever he was around, the girls flocked, but not to us hot jet pilots. Nope, they were always captivated by Bill's smile. He had blindingly white teeth, hair as black as midnight, and he always dressed like a gentleman. He would have been a perfect Las Vegas Maitre d.' A wise colonel once told me to find a good top sergeant to teach me the ropes in SAC before I got "SACumcised." Although it was against regulations for enlisted men and officers to fraternize, the rule was generally overlooked on SAC's B-52 crews. Bill and I, being the only bachelors on the crew, became friends. It was inevitable. We didn't tell anybody but it seemed natural. And the girls he introduced me to—well, his scraps were better than most men's feasts.

Mather Air Force Base (pronounced May-ther) was considered the finest duty assignment in all of SAC. Located on the east side of Sacramento, California, in the heart of Gold Strike Country, it was considered a "warm" assignment as opposed to most other SAC bases strung out along our northern border. There is probably nothing wrong with being stationed at Glasgow AFB, Montana, but I heard the people who lived there thought nothing of driving 250 miles to get to Minot AFB, North Dakota, for a weekend of fun. Only one problem: the good people of Minot thought nothing of taking that same weekend to drive 200 miles to Grand Forks AFB, which is still north of Fargo. And snowmobiles had not yet been invented!

It was all too cold for me. At Mather, we were only two hours from San Francisco and two hours from Lake Tahoe, take your pick. Somehow, the driving time of two hours seemed infinitely less than 120 miles. That's California thinking.

Life on the alert pad quickly got boring. Oh, there were exceedingly interesting things to do and very intelligent people to discuss ideas with. We constantly studied top secret targets and ways to get to them, along with fascinating things about the world of war, nukes, enemies, their defenses, important news events and related intelligence, but damn, after a while it all got boring. The routine of life on the pad kept us busy during the day doing this interesting stuff, but when normal families were getting together in the evening, we just sat around with a bunch of other guys and none of us could even go to the fridge for a beer!

Some of the guys read or studied in their rooms or did mission planning with the navigators—man, I'm sure glad I was never a navigator. Others watched TV or played pool or joined the ongoing, big-time game of Risk in one of the crew study rooms. However, the best place to spend an evening was in our small library, large enough that seven or eight guys could squeeze themselves in, most sitting on the floor, to listen to the banter of Dennis McGrath and Jim Kinney, two EWO's who got into the wildest discussions of anything you might want to hear. McGrath was Boston

Irish and Kinney was New York obnoxious, so if the subject was baseball, you can imagine the battle between the Red Sox and Yankees. But these guys made it fun, mixing sarcasm with intelligence and a bit of grace to keep the edge off. At the time I thought of writing down some of what they said, but it all came in such a stream that I just sat back and enjoyed.

The library discussions always started out seriously with subjects such as important developments in the day's events, like the Cold War or the progress of America's space program. But usually it degenerated into a bitch session about SAC's "infinite wisdom" or about some vengeful staff officer and then it spun off into a McGrath/Kinney comedy special until lights out. I loved it all except for the fact that while we were on alert I felt like a prisoner in a scientifically designed gilded cage.

Alert tours lasted either three or four days with changeover on Monday and Friday mornings. Everyone was in his crew order seat at 0700 sharp for weather, intelligence, and staff briefings. Then we'd go out to the planes and changeover the "GO" codes, a ritual procedure that was exceptionally secure. If we finished changeover early we could get a bite of breakfast in the mess hall, the m-m-most delicious food in the military. The rest of the first morning on alert we spent studying our particular combat mission and all the tiny details including everything from the exact length of our takeoff to the distance we'd roll out upon landing with and without a drag chute. Much of this seemed kind of redundant until you realized it all fit together into a plan. In fact, the top-secret plan was called the Single Integrated Operations Plan, the SIOP, which contained everything one needed to know to fight a complete nuclear war. Sorry, I don't discuss details.

Every single alert tour we got the Klaxon. The Klaxon is the loudest thing that mankind has ever invented. If someone were to record a perfectly resonant fart, then turned the volume to about 50 decibels above a rock band's maximum output (which is louder than a B-52 taking off) and gave you a series of two-second blasts—only then could you understand what the Klaxon sounded like. The thing could go off at any time of the day or night and would damn well wake the dead; it was a real adrenaline rush that could damage your hearing. In one-tenth of a second all hell would break loose as everyone jumped up and ran for their planes.

The ramps out of the alert pad exploded with men running at top speed. The first crewman to reach our bomber opened the hatch, and the first pilot into the cockpit hit the cartridge start button on engine number two. While the engine spooled up, we'd strap in and as soon as it reached 70 percent power, I'd connect an alternator to give us electrical power so the radios would come on line. Then we'd use bleed-air from engine two to start the other engines, and by the time they reached idle power, the navigators and EW would give us confirmation whether to immediately take off and go to war . . . or not. Of course, all of this was just a game because we knew we were not going to war with nuclear bombs aboard unless the world situation had already deteriorated to nonsense. The world situation was forever nonsensical so there was always an element of doubt.

In reality, since we were kept abreast of every little thing going on in the world, we felt there was no chance of the nuke battle flag going up without something else happening first. All that Doctor Strangelove stuff was funny, but I thought it was pure bull until I realized people in the real world believed in movies like that because we truly did not inform them of much. SAC was a secret society where we lived in enclosed, guarded areas and flew great big airplanes that carried nuclear bombs and missiles.

In their ignorance, writers and movie makers let their imaginations run wild. They thought everyone would enjoy seeing guys who were nuts playing with nukes like they were toys. My experience from the very first day proved that nobody joked around because the peace of the entire world was, literally, at stake. Any aircrew member who acted a little bit crazy, even one time, was gone! And yet, we were all crazy for putting up with it. Catch-22, anyone? Or was it Catch-23, exactly the opposite? None of us were ever certain which.

We got adept at guessing when the Klaxon would go off and it often became a topic of conversation in the library, until McGrath and Kinney took over. Changeover days were mostly peaceful. The top brass usually did not sound the Klaxon because we had a lot of secret stuff lying around in the crew study rooms. Of course, it would take an idiot to try and get into the pad to steal some of it as the place was guarded tighter than Fort Knox. Even with all the idiots in the world, they were at least smart enough to know better than to try. In the entire history of SAC, I don't think anybody ever seriously tried to sneak into an alert facility. Please, the military always excuses us second lieutenants—if only for being plain dumb.

When that damned Klaxon sounded we always hoped it would be a "Bravo" alert as opposed to a "Coco." With the Bravo we only started the engines, copied the Go code message, confirmed it, and then shut down the engines and topped off the fuel tanks. The Coco alert meant we had to fast-taxi to the runway and pretend to take off, rolling down the runway with our engines at full power for only a few seconds, then back to idle. After that it was an elephant walk around the base with eight big bombers each following the guy in front back to the alert pad.

It was really important to be the first in line during a Coco Exercise because it meant that when it was finished, you got to park on the Christmas tree hardstand right beside the alert pad. Therefore, you had the shortest distance to run for the next Klaxon. A Coco always took a couple of hours to complete and there was usually a maintenance problem to cope with that required the pilots to remain in the cockpit until it was repaired. That might take all day and if we didn't have the foresight to bring a magazine or book to read, well, it could get very boring. Looking back on it now I just can't imagine why it seemed so boring. The very serious "fun and games" harassment to keep us on our toes was fascinating, but boooring because we always waited for something that we knew would probably never happen . . . nuclear war.

We did our mission planning in the squadron building, an old, World War II barracks converted for our use. Mission planning required a full day to complete and it seemed there was a form for everything. Bill Hart always said, "When the gross weight of the paperwork equals the gross weight of the airplane, you're cleared for takeoff!"

My job was to compute all the takeoff data, airspeeds, distance, fuel, and weapons weights and such. That took about half an hour. Then I worked on the fuel curve, the copilot's primary job. The B-52F carried well over 300,000 pounds of jet fuel and it had to be burned out in a definite sequence in order to keep the plane in balance. We called that balance "cg" for center of gravity (and throughout this story you'll notice I did a lot of bitching about the fuel curve). When I finished planning the fuel curve I was free to be the gofer for the whole crew. Lunch, anyone?

Our standard training missions were eight to twelve hours in the air depending on what we had to do to fill all the squares in each crew member's annual training folder. Our "Local Flying Area" was the entire western half of the United States. With navigation legs that lasted two hours and using aerial refueling we crisscrossed the country more than a few times during each flight.

We dropped small marking bombs on ranges as diverse as the Boardman Range in Washington State to the Matamoros Island Range off the coast of Texas in the Gulf of Mexico. There was also an array of radar "bomb plots" scattered across the country where we dropped radio "tones." I know that must sound silly but that's what we did—drop tones. These bomb plots had radars that could track our B-52's very accurately and they could determine where any type of bomb would land if it was released exactly when the aircraft bombing system "broke" a radio tone. They could do this on any number of targets with us flying at high, medium, or low altitudes, and then give us our bombing scores in feet from the target within seconds of our tone release.

In the B-52 one of the copilot's minor jobs was to run the two Ultra High Frequency (UHF) radios. One radio was usually tuned in to Air Traffic Control, the other we could use to contact one of the bomb plots. Three sites we used a lot were the Saint George Bomb Plot in Utah, the Hawthorne Bomb Plot in Nevada, and the Wilder Bomb Plot in Idaho. At Wilder once, I screwed up the radios and we dropped a tone on the Boise Sector of Seattle Center. Of course, this didn't affect Air Traffic Control except that they had a radio tone for several seconds on their primary control frequency for Boise. Wilder Bomb Plot, after all these years, is still awaiting the tone break of our B-52 because it never came and we were credited with a "bad" bomb, thanks to some copilot who got his radios mixed up.

A bad bomb was considered a very bad thing in SAC. It meant your crew was stupid and should work harder to prevent these things from happening. We had to go before the Bad Bomb Review Board and everyone got to know why crew E-06 not only missed their target but also that there was a real dumb copilot on that crew. I was saved by the fact that every other copilot in the wing was just as dumb as me and that it took time to work out these kinks. I guess it's kind of like a lineman jumping offside during a football game. He really feels stupid for a while—until the next play . . . so life goes on.

Most of the time in the air during these butt-numbing training flights was spent on navigation legs. There were several types of navigation and our navigators had to practice all of them during the course of a training year. Celestial navigation was where the EWO used a sextant to give the navigators star information, and they figured out where we were at from that, just like Columbus and Magellan but with a modern sextant. Our Hound Dog missiles had an Astrotracker, which the navigators practiced with as a backup. Of course, dead reckoning was the basic form of navigation. They also used radar navigation, which mapped the land below and guided us to any target selected by the radar navigator. There were several other styles of navigation that only the navigators knew about. I could usually tell where we were by looking down at Denver or

Salt Lake City or by checking the TACAN (tactical air navigation system) or VOR (VHF omnidirectional radio range) position in our cockpit. The reason navigators needed so much practice with their strange methods was because there were no TACAN or VOR navigation stations north of the Arctic Circle, and Russia certainly wasn't going to provide us with any help in finding their targets.

The Hound Dog was the first cruise missile, and we usually carried one under each wing. As one of my copilot duties, I got to start their engines and control them during flight. Actually, all I had was a little wafer knob that went clockwise to run the engines up and counterclockwise to turn them down and off. Big deal, but it made me feel kind of important to report to the navigators that "I have the starboard missile ready for launch." I just turned the wafer knob to cruise, big deal.

Each "nav leg" lasted about two hours and we flew a couple of them on each mission. Sometimes we used the Astrotracker computer in the Hound Dog missiles to guide us, as if our systems in the plane had quit and the missile was all we had remaining for navigation. We'd fly a two-hour nav leg with it, and then pretend to launch the missile at Dallas or Chicago. If all the war games SAC played during the Cold War had been done with real bombs, there would be nothing left of the planet, much less of Dallas or Chicago.

Somewhere during every training mission we met up with a flying gas station to get some fuel. Air Traffic Control would guide us to a KC-135 tanker, Jim Gehrig would nuzzle up underneath the thing, and the tanker's boom operator would stick this red, yellow, and green tube into a refueling receptacle on top of our plane behind the cockpit. Then we'd sit there while the tanker pumped a lot of jet fuel into us. My job was to direct that fuel into our gas tanks in a certain sequence in order to keep our "cg" correct. After refueling I always had a handful of other duties: make sure Jim cleared the tanker safely, tell Air Traffic Control of our intentions, give the gunner an oxygen check, and then write everything into the fuel log.

The most fun we had on any of our training missions was when we got to be targets for Air Defense Command's F-101's that flew out of Hamilton and Klamath Falls air defense bases. We flew racetrack patterns over the stunning vistas of Northern California and Southern Oregon while the F-101's chased us up and down the coast. Except for the thirty-degree bank turns at each end of the racetrack pattern, we were supposed to maintain straight and level flight at 40,000 feet. The B-52 has a gigantic wing and, in the thin air at high altitude, we could still maneuver better than anything else that ever flew.

The gunner would sit backwards in the tail of the B-52 a couple of hundred feet behind us and his job was to pretend to shoot at the fighters coming in. Then the fighters pretended to shoot missiles and guns at us and so the whole procedure was a standoff for everyone in order to fill their annual training squares. All this drove Bill Neville nuts. One time he told us that he wanted to do a hard turn into the fighter when it was almost in position to fire at us. When he said, "Now!" Jim Gehrig turned into the fighter using 45 degrees of bank. At 40,000 feet that is a lot because there is almost no air at that altitude to hold an airplane up. The F-101 driver must have been a second lieutenant, like me, because he overshot trying to keep up with our turn and fell several thousand feet. We never saw him again. I secretly hoped he'd have to meet something like our Bad Bomb Board to explain why he was dumber than a B-52 crew.

By then it was time to head for the barn. We pilots were already tired from eight to ten hours of busy flying—but, in fact, we hadn't yet done any real flying. Except for the takeoff and the aerial refueling, which were flown by Jim Gehrig, the autopilot had done all the flying for us. I was busy running and monitoring most of the aircraft's systems while Jim kept watch over everything to ensure none of us made any mistakes. Since Jim did the takeoff, I got to make the descent, approach, and landing.

Hand flying the B-52 is exceptionally hard work, especially for me because I am quite short and only weighed about 120 pounds at the time. Regardless, the B-52 is a pig to fly! There, I said it. She's huge and requires a lot of muscle just to haul her ass around the sky. Those massive wings create stability and that means muscular effort just to turn the yoke. In pilot training I won a small trophy for being the jock of the class (because of my diminutive size and the fact that I had almost no body fat), but even that didn't help when trying to move that mother around the sky. Like an ex-wife, she fought you all the way.

However, when it had to, the B-52 could drop out of the sky faster than a hawk diving on a field mouse. On top of both wings were spoilers, hydraulically activated panels, which could destroy almost all the aerodynamic lift on the wings. When they were raised full up to the "Airbrakes Six" position, the airplane could fall thousands of feet in a matter of seconds—and yet it remained in full control.

We never used Airbrakes Six during training at Mather but I had witnessed the maneuver from the cockpit, so that I'd know how it was done, during my initial B-52 checkout at Castle Air Force Base. To demonstrate, the instructor pilot flew into the traffic pattern around 1500 feet above the runway until he was about a quarter mile out. Then he went to airbrakes six for a few seconds. We immediately dropped 1500 feet and landed pretty much where we were supposed to land, on the approach end of the runway. Some demonstration! I almost needed to change my flight suit right there! If an airline pilot could do that with an airliner there would be a plane full of heart attacks, and any survivors would be found running for the rest rooms.

Whenever I got to hand fly the B-52, I always kicked the lever that let the rudders out full and I moved my ejection seat down as close to the yoke as I could get it. Still, flying that hog had me all splayed out. It was a stretch just to get my feet on the rudders, hold onto that yoke, and then try to get my left hand around those eight throttles and still see over the dashboard. My hand was not large enough to fit around all the throttles, so when I needed to move them I learned the trick of "twist and wiggle" with my wrist so as to move all eight of them a bit at a time.

An instrument penetration is a precise letdown from high altitude to a runway's final approach for landing. Every Air Force base, and all major airports, publish at least one penetration. At Mather we had all the headings, turns, and altitudes memorized but it was still a chore to bring that baby home. She fought us every mile of the way in, and by the time we were ready for landing the guy flying was usually half worn out.

Landing the B-52 is a hoot. There is no other airplane like it in the whole world. Further, it requires a 300-foot-wide runway because of the outrigger landing gear under the wing tips. When a normal airplane lands in a cross wind, the pilot can dip a wing and use some opposite rudder to stay lined up with the runway. But, how do you dip a wing when it's nearly a block long? You don't! Unique to the B-52 is a system where we can lift up this knob behind the throttles and twist it to dial in what we need to land in a crosswind. What this does is turn the four landing gear trucks so as to align them with the runway and then we fly down final approach sideways. And the B-52 lands that way—sideways!

In three years of flying the B-52, my chief worry was that I might accidentally get the landing gear trucks aligned backwards. Then, instead of the trucks being straight with the runway for landing, they would be twice as far misaligned the opposite way. If they were misaligned when we touched down, the plane would be headed down the runway but the landing gear would be aimed out into left field. When you are flying something the size of a whole city block, it can get a bit unnerving, so I checked the landing gear several times before every landing.

In early August of 1964, just after I arrived at Mather, there were a couple of incidents in the Gulf of Tonkin, south of China, that alerted our intelligence people. They briefed us thoroughly about it. The news reports were sketchy, and intel didn't have much more to say except that a young U.S. Navy lieutenant named Everett Alvarez got shot down on a retaliation strike and was being held as a war criminal in a place called Hanoi, North Vietnam. He was my age. This incident didn't have much to do with us since we were a nuclear force, so most of us kind of ignored it as one of those Cold War things that kept happening. Within a month the 320th Bomb Wing quietly received orders to begin training with conventional "iron bombs," the kind they used in World War II. With that order, we became the first bomb wing in SAC to have the "dual commitment" of being qualified with both nukes and conventional bombs.

Chapter Two

Every B-52 wing in the Strategic Air Command was required to pull a month of Chrome Dome flying about once a year. Chrome Dome was the military code name for airborne nuclear alert missions over the Arctic. America kept a number of B-52's, fully loaded with nuclear bombs and missiles, airborne around the clock 24 hours a day for three decades. During this era of the Cold War there was NEVER a moment that we did not have nuclear bombs in the air, ready to strike our primary opponents, the Soviet Union and China. The Cold War was real and far more serious than most Americans ever knew.

America's nuclear deterrent force was three pronged and known as the Triad. It consisted of nuclear tipped Intercontinental Ballistic Missiles, Polaris and Poseidon class nuclear submarines and, of course, the B-52's. We kept thousands of nuclear bombs in various stages of alert, ready for instant delivery to the communists should they preemptively strike our homeland. I became a part of this by joining the Air Force two weeks after the Cuban Missile Crisis. President Kennedy was assassinated a year later while I was in pilot training. The world was living on a hair trigger and we, in the Triad, were the bullets.

The 320th Bomb Wing's annual Chrome Dome responsibility rolled around and we had to launch one B-52 every day for a month. Each bomber carried nuclear bombs and missiles up over the North Pole and remained on airborne alert for 24 hours of the 28-hour mission. Did I say 28 hours? Numb butt time! Numb butt time! Did you ever try to sit in church on a hard pew for 28 straight hours? There is no crying in baseball! And there is no whining in SAC! You can bitch all you want but do it in the library while you are on alert.

Bill Hart told us that the "goat," the lowest-ranking man academically in each graduating class at the military academies of West Point, Annapolis, and Colorado Springs, was assigned to the Pentagon for one year as punishment for being last in his class. The goats' sole duty was to think up nicknames for military operations. He said that was how they came up with the name "Chrome Dome," as in shiny bald pate of the world.

When we pulled airborne nuclear alert duty, there was no letup in the number of planes we kept on ground alert; our wing's mission requirement remained at eight. We simply incorporated the Chrome Dome missions into our regular training schedule and our extra duties were reduced to basically zero. Chrome Dome was real world and nuclear serious.

Our crew's turn in the pickle barrel rolled around and we didn't have to do a minute of mission planning as it had already been done for us. The fuel curve had been fine tuned by countless missions already flown. However, we spent considerable time studying the mission on the alert pad the day prior to the flight. Takeoff was at 0700 and that meant a "get up" at three o'clock in the morning. We slept on the alert pad, where our B-52 was being prepared for the mission out on the Christmas tree.

Three o'clock comes early no matter what your profession—and the gunner was grouchy. I dozed through breakfast in the mess hall and zombied my way through the last-minute briefings, trying to keep notes on what I thought was important. It didn't matter, everything had been done a zillion times before and all we had to do was be robots for the next day and a half. We could follow a flip-chart checklist that contained almost everything we needed to know from frequencies to points of interest along the route. Of course, most of that information was classified.

The airplane was bathed in artificial light. People and vehicles rushed around making sure everything was ready for our arrival. Once we loaded our bags into the plane and stuffed our stuff wherever it would fit—the design engineers never, even in today's modern airplanes, made a special place large enough for a pilot to put his stuff—we did the preflight. For some long-forgotten reason that predates World War II and its B-17's and B-24's, tradition had it that during the exterior preflight of the airplane, the copilot inspects the pilot's side and the pilot inspects the copilot's side. Just walking around one side of a B-52 looking for leaks, missing flaps, and holes in the side of the fuselage was a week's worth of exercise for a couch potato. The airplane was ready.

The cockpit was awash in red lighting to keep our night vision intact. Cooling air from an external ground unit whooshed through the cockpit with such a racket that it prevented speech except over the interphone. The B-52's design engineers placed a bunch of windows around the cockpit and again tradition called for a window on each side to open so the pilots could stick their heads out and holler something to somebody on the ground. It had to be another holdover from the B-17. Why we needed this in an airplane capable of flying at over 50,000 feet, I'll never know, but it created a large window well where we put all our checklists, clipboards, maps, box lunches, and other stuff. During flight both pilots' window wells were always overflowing with stuff.

We got on with the silent part of our checklist. The navigators inspected the bombs and the missiles and, finally, someone closed the entry hatch. Upstairs, we could always tell when the hatch was closed because there was an abrupt change in air pressure and, with it closed, we found ourselves isolated and working as a team. The interphone began to crackle as everyone checked in and I realized I was finally awake after three hours of sleepwalking. I called out the checklist, Jim Gehrig responded, and we started all eight engines and spent the next half hour thoroughly checking all the systems in the airplane.

The crew chief on the ground coordinated everything with us over the interphone. We moved the flaps up and down, and he told us that they moved up and down. Then we moved all the control surfaces and again, he told us what moved and where. He stayed on interphone with us until we were ready to taxi. Some of the most important people in the Air Force—always has been, always will be—are aircraft maintenance people. They never get much word play but pilots love them. Crew chiefs are assigned their own airplane and they take great pride in keeping it perfectly airworthy.

There were ten hydraulic packs that thrummed loudly throughout the plane whenever they came on line. One pack operated each of four landing gear trucks, and others moved control surfaces on each wing and in the tail. As these came on line our B-52 began to come alive. I often thought how this huge machine resembled the human body: an aircrew for the brain, pumps for the heart, hydraulics for muscles, electronics for a nervous system, radios to communicate, and so on. With everything up and running and with a good aircrew working together, the B-52 almost became a living thing. We always referred to the B-52 in female terms, probably because sometimes she could get real temperamental.

Moving that great big, silver, air-sucking B-52F on the ground didn't take much throttle, but a bit too much could blow down a small building behind the plane if you didn't use care. Once the chocks were removed and the brakes were released it took only a small power shot with the throttles to get us moving. Then the B-52 would coast along right smartly. Both of us pilots kept our eyeballs roving while security trucks led and trailed us toward the runway. She taxied just about like any other airplane except that she was big and weighed well over 200 tons. It was a little like dancing with the fat lady—a bit slow to get up to speed, but what inertia. We were always saying 'clear left' or 'clear right' whenever anything like a flight line vehicle or a building got too near the wing tip. "Whoa! Thet buildin' thar on th' raht jest jumped out et us!"

There was a small (what am I saying here? nothing about any of this was small) parking area near the end of the runway where we could stop and go over last minute items. Exactly one minute before takeoff, Terry began counting each ten seconds and gave us a countdown from ten so that we crossed the runway hold line "on the hack" with universal BBC time, broadcast from Greenwich, England. SAC liked to do everything by the count, and they ran this railroad with everyone exactly on time all the time.

As we crossed the hold line, Terry yelled, "Go!" and Jim brought the throttles up to about 70 percent while I turned the wafer switches on the missiles to 100 percent power. He danced the fat lady onto the runway and pushed the throttles to full power, then gave them to me. I increased throttle friction a bit and held them full forward. The rush we got as we accelerated down the runway began to seep into the bones of all of us. The dashboard instruments came to life and all the engine instruments pegged themselves to maximum power. The airspeed indicator came off its peg at 60 knots and Terry called out a line speed known as "S-One." He hacked a clock, waited an appropriate time, and called, "S-Two! Line speed's good." The plane began to buck a bit as it picked up speed and the wings began to fly.

Now, the wings on a B-52 actually do fly . . . I mean apart from the airplane itself. On the ground and heavy with fuel, the wings droop so much that even I can reach up and touch the tips, but on the runway, as they begin to generate lift, the wing tips actually rise about 30 feet! That's three stories on a tall building! The tallest building in my hometown was six stories, and that's how tall our tail was. When the wings got to full up and the airspeed was right, I called, "Unstick!" and Jim pulled back slightly on the yoke. That leviathan of the air lifted off the ground just like any small Cessna.

I held the throttles at full power and when we got to about 100 feet altitude, Jim raised the landing gear handle. Four hydraulic packs came on line and lifted each gear truck into its wheel well. The two outrigger landing gear that held up the wing tips on the ground also lifted themselves into their respective wheel wells. When the six landing gears were up and locked and after we had accelerated some more I raised the flaps to 15 percent and then to full up. About this time, the 10,000 pounds of water injection, which had been squirted into the engines to increase air density for extra thrust, ran dry. It was like coming out of afterburner in a fighter; things got quieter in the cockpit as we coasted up to climb speed.

Jet noise! The sound of freedom! The roar is music to me, and I realize it may not be pleasant for everyone, but I've always been fascinated just watching airplanes fly.

I don't know if we woke anybody up in Sacramento but we turned away from the city onto the "Jackson 5 Departure" to climb toward the Sierra Nevada Mountains. I was really busy during this time running the checklist, the radios and the fuel system, but I always managed a few peeks at the beauty of those mountains as they fell away below us. We kept turning and climbing until we reached 35,000 feet and leveled off, staying away from all populated areas. Hey, we were carrying a bunch of nukes and people didn't expect them to fall on their heads—so we avoided people. In fact, Sacramento was the last populated area we'd see until we returned from flying around much of the northern hemisphere.

Sitting in the cockpit of a B-52, a pilot cannot see the nose of the airplane. Windows surround the pilot, and the feeling is like going up and down in a tall, outside elevator. In a fighter the nose gets pointed up or down or even sideways. In a B-52 the nose seems to stay on one keel—but this particular elevator doesn't stop until it reaches heaven.

At level off, I called Oakland Center to tell them we were at our cruise altitude, then I called the gunner for an oxygen check (he was still grouchy), and finally I logged the fuel. Every tank read exactly what it was supposed to. Jim and I didn't talk much during flight, leaving the interphone open mostly to hear anything important. We did signal each other a lot and we understood this pilot shorthand that every crew developed as its own internal communication. We constantly watched all the instruments, our eyes flitting over the primary ones—the attitude indicator, navigation instruments, and the engine instruments—about once per minute. We still had a lot of time to sit back and watch the world go by. It was truly beautiful.

We coasted out over the Pacific Ocean near Ukiah and turned northwest toward Alaska. Things quickly got routine. Every three or four hours one of us pilots would get out of our seat to go downstairs and harass the navigators, take a leak in the standpipe, and stretch our stiff bodies. Terry was always sitting in the radar navigator's seat playing with the radar, and Bill Hart was usually asleep in the navigator's seat with his cheek resting on his right palm and his elbow balanced on the navigator's worktable. I don't know how he slept that way, but during this mission I believe he got a couple of nights' worth of sleep.

Jim Erbes, the electronic warfare officer, sat about twenty feet behind the pilots in a cubbyhole full of high tech electronics. Every time I passed him he was asleep with his oxygen mask dangling from his face and yet whenever he was needed or called over the interphone, he was right there. One time when I was wandering around, I stuck a fresh stick of gum into his snoring mouth and then hustled back to my seat. He didn't notice.

Flying up on Alaska at 45,000 feet, the vista of a brilliant-white, mountainous world stretched away as far as I could see. Below, on our right, lay the wilds of one of the highest mountain systems in North America, the rugged St. Elias Range, which appeared almost flat from our altitude. Alaska and the Yukon were a virgin white, streaked with blue and violet hues. This panorama seemed infinite as it stretched into an unverifiable horizon that blended into a very bright, light-blue sky that darkened slightly into the outer space above us. It was one of the most beautiful sights I've ever seen in my life. Robert Service called this land "the Polar Zone" in his poem "To the Man of the High North."

We coasted in on southern Alaska about 50 miles west of the Canadian border and descended to 30,000 feet to enter the Cold Coffee East Aerial Refueling Track—the ensigns and second lieutenants in the Pentagon got "cold coffee" right. KC-135 tankers, stationed at Eielson Air Force Base in Fairbanks, climbed up to meet us and to transfer every drop of gas they had available. They off-loaded 6,000 pounds of jet fuel per minute, and it took 30 minutes for the transfer! I logged it all and we were 180,000 pounds heavier. That's a lot of gas—about 28,000 gallons!

When we dropped off the tanker and climbed back up to cruise altitude, everything outside the cockpit became a dense gray that got darker by the mile. As clear and bright as it was in the sunlight, there was a murkiness in the twilight of the Arctic. It was like flying into a dense fog that slowly envelops you, like something unknown out of a horror movie. Suddenly, and I mean suddenly, everything outside turned midnight black and after a few seconds little dots of starlight popped out everywhere. My eyes beheld all the stars that ever were. And then, for the first time in my life, I saw the Aurora Borealis. Stunning! Awesome! There are no words to describe . . .

The Aurora, far in the distance, massive; I could not determine its altitude. It was the sheerest fabric of turquoise, and hung from the heavens like an expensive drapery cut precisely at the bottom and hemmed perfectly. It coursed completely across our wind-screen and appeared to go clear around the Arctic, which it did. The top of the Aurora was uneven with streaks that extended far into space. I came to understand that the Aurora Borealis has an exact mirror image during the same instant in the Antarctic called the Aurora Australis. The streaks of charged particles coming in from the sun hit the earth's magnetic field and align themselves equally on both poles of the Earth. And they shine. And in color.

As we left the North Slope of Alaska, still heading straight for the North Pole, Terry broke a long silence on the interphone, "Pilot, Nav, if you maintain this heading for the next six hours or so, we'll fly directly over downtown Moscow!"

"Really?" I said.

"That's not our route!" said Jim.

"That's right Pilot, we're going to switch to Grid Navigation in a couple of minutes. Just thought I'd warn you."

"Rog."

A couple of minutes later all the navigation indicators in our cockpit started spinning and finally settled on a heading that was certainly not true north. Then Terry told us to turn right to a heading of something like west, which didn't make sense. We turned, and within an hour I was lost, without a clue as to where we were or where we were going. Before that moment, I'd always had an exceptional sense of direction. I lost that feeling, that internal anchor that got me everywhere from the grocery store to a new base across the country, and it remained like that for the next twelve hours or so. I knew enough that I could find the Big Dipper, Orion, and the North Star, but when you think about it, the North Star, Polaris, was almost directly above us and I could see it through my ejection-hatch window. The Big Dipper, Ursa Major, was going around the world in the opposite direction from us, only twice as fast. If you're an astronomer, maybe you can figure all this out, I couldn't. Before long I wasn't sure if we were north of

Greenland, Norway, or Siberia. Even the Magnetic North Pole was far to the south of us.

I took a break and went downstairs to see where we were on the navigator's Grid maps. Terry's maps were solid white with groups of colored lines on them. It didn't mean a thing to me except that if the maps were white they must indicate the icecap we were flying over. On my way back to my seat I saw that Jim Erbes was awake, smiling and chewing gum. I waved and chuckled to myself about the secret that only I knew.

Outside the airplane, at 45,000 feet, the temperature was something around 60 degrees below zero. The temperature on the icecap was about the same or colder. If something bad happened and we had to eject, we would be frozen tuna long before our parachutes hit the icecap with our corpses. The nearest base was Thule, Greenland, somewhere far to the south, whichever way that was because, essentially, every direction was south.

Our B-52 droned on. Every half hour I gave the gunner oxygen checks, as required, and every time I had to awaken him. He was always grouchy. The fuel curve showed we were practically making our own gas in the thin air of near space. Jet engines are very efficient at high altitude and we were above about 95 percent of the earth's atmosphere.

For hours I was in complete awe, never expecting the top of our world to reveal itself like it was now doing for me. There was absolutely no sunlight that reached this far north at this time of year. We flew on through the subdued darkness of the earth's umbra. There was no moon. Like the sun, it was hidden by the earth itself. When we were not flying near the Aurora, the only light was from starlight and it reflected off the white world below with enough lumens to read by! This ghostly scene of blacks, grays, and pinpoints of starlight was downright eerie. It stretched on and on.

Occasionally, we flew under the Aurora, which remained a continuous fascination for me. We cruised at 45,000 feet, about nine miles up, yet the Aurora's drapery seemed like it was ten times higher than we were flying. From below, it revealed turquoise folds that curved in a most delicate manner, stretching farther into the heavens than I could imagine. I could go into the scientific mode to describe this but that would take away from the artistic beauty of the far north that very few have ever seen. It made me feel insignificant.

This huge airplane we were flying, with its unbelievable array of weapons, was but nothing in the wilderness of what I could see in the polar sky. We could have dropped all of our nuclear bombs here and, if the explosions were not discovered by seismographs and radiation detectors, no one ever would have known. The Polar Zone is so vast you could lose the entire United States, including Alaska, up there. Then you could throw in Europe and still have lots of room left over—and that would cover only the Arctic Ocean. It takes most of Siberia and most of Canada to fill the rest of the Polar Zone.

Terry warned us when we approached Russia. Bill Neville actually woke up and monitored the tail area during our entire flight north of the Soviet Sector but we remained well out of fighter range. Jim Erbes was glued to his instruments, listening for any radar that might be tracking us. He reported the odd click of each long-range radar as the Soviets began to monitor us. They watched us very closely, knowing exactly where we were and when we'd be somewhere else. They also knew that if they decided to start a war, our B-52 would immediately disappear from their radars and, within a short time, so would great chunks of their own country. Pundits and politicians called all of this "brinkmanship," and maybe it was, but the fact remains that we held them off for over two generations and the Cold War never developed into World War III.

Being in a lone warplane above the icecap north of Russia is a very uncomfortable feeling. We were now at the tip of the Cold War spear. I remembered reading in *Life* magazine during the late 1950s about a B-47 that strayed a bit too close to Russia in this area. It got shot down and the crew was "rescued" by the Russians. A couple of the men, named McCone and Olmstead, were held in the Kremlin's notorious Lubyanka Political Prison in Moscow. Eventually, they were exchanged for Soviet spies and McCone later became the commandant of the Air Force Survival Training Center at Stead Air Force Base near Reno, Nevada.

One of the basic requirements of everyone who flew in SAC was to live through about a month of arctic survival training at Stead. After I had earned the Silver Wings of an

Air Force pilot, SAC told me, and others, that if we didn't pass the survival course they would legally take away our wings and send us to some remote duty spot at the end of the earth. SAC was serious about this, like they were about everything. So I survived Stead only because I wanted to keep my wings and I certainly did not want to spend my career at some radar site in northern Alaska.

Stead had a realistic Prisoner of War camp, fully equipped and with guards who had defected from several communist countries. They had developed numerous torture techniques that did not actually harm us; however, their methods were diabolical and cruel. It was nothing compared to the real torture we could expect in a real communist prison camp anywhere in the world, but they did want to see how much crap we could take.

What I remember best about my experience in the Stead POW camp was secreting 96 small American flags into the camp taped inside the toes of my boots. My old pilot training buddy Bobby Grabstald was my roommate in the Bachelor Officer's Quarters at Stead and while I was making the flags with red and blue magic markers, he was dressing after a shower. He said, "Hey, I want to wear one of those flags, paint one on my chest."

"They'll see it there and use it against you," I said.

"Okay, do it under my shorts, they won't look there." He dropped the back of his shorts a bit so I made a few marks high on his backside beneath the band on his underwear. Both of us were super patriots and were not thinking of any disrespect toward our nation's flag. Then he wanted "US Gov't Inspected" on the other side as sort of a joke. I complied and we both forgot about it. It was to be our first object lesson in the deception, lies, and spin that communists used in order to persuade and control great groups of people throughout the world. A misguided patriotic act would be turned into a nightmare for Bobby.

That night, 96 of us crawled about a mile through a simulated minefield until we were "captured." When they caught us, we began the POW experience. Immediately, they stripped us naked and searched our clothes for contraband. The real, ex-communist guards couldn't help laughing at Grabstald's rear and they took a Polaroid photo of it. Then they threw us into tiny cells three feet by three feet by three feet. Being quite small, I was comfortable but it was late February and excessively cold. Besides the flags, I had smuggled about 50 birthday candles and some matches into the camp by threading them into the drawstrings on my field jacket. They were ineffective in warding off the bitter cold.

After three or four days and nights of isolation (they played time tricks on us) and simulated torture (which damned well seemed real), we were thrown into a compound together. Ninety-six of us were herded into a crude, covered dugout where I distributed one of the small flags to each of the grizzled-looking, simulated Prisoners of War. Everyone seemed to appreciate getting a flag of his own, a reminder that what we were doing was for a purpose larger than ourselves alone. Shortly afterward, we were called out into the open compound and lined up for a communist lecture. It was sometime in the middle of the night and very cold.

Captain McCone, who had suffered for real at his communist captors' hands in the notorious Lubyanka, stood in front of us screeching like they had done to him—and he called forth poor Grabstald. McCone then proceeded to give him communist hell for desecrating an American flag. All the while I'm standing in formation doing everything I can to keep from busting out laughing. I coughed constantly to cover my laughter while Grabs suffered in front of the formation. Ninety-five of us were giggling in church and coughing to cover it up. When it was all over Grabstald refused to talk about it, ever. Sorry, Bobby, I still think it was funny—and none of us were laughing at you—but it drove home a powerful point for all of us, that anything could be twisted by communist lies and that some people could actually be influenced by the spin.

After a week of freezing POW training I thought I could never again get that cold. But I soon found out I was wrong. They took us into the mountains about 20 miles north of the Donner Pass to a place about 2,000 feet higher in elevation. It was still winter and well below freezing all day long! We had no food to speak of, only one sardine tin of compressed, tasteless survival food that was supposed to last us a week. In the High Sierra we were taught how to survive those conditions with almost nothing to eat, a

50-pound backpack and snowshoes. Then they chased us all over the Sierra Nevada Mountains, day and night! I was barely tall enough to get into pilot training and, unlike today, had almost no body fat to help me keep warm. It was so cold that we all stayed awake the last night of training and built a large bonfire. We melted snow in canteen cups and made what we called Manzanita Tea from the bushes of the High Sierra. Yuk!

My trek mate during this week was Second Lieutenant Michael James Patrick Rooney—an Irishman. He wore John Elway's toothy smile, and he peeped out from under a four-flap winter hat that made us all look like Chinese communists. Over the years we became good friends, and we had remarkably similar Air Force careers. We not only survived the Stead Survival School together, we also attended Nuclear Weapons School and B-52 checkout, and much later, went through F-111 checkout together. More important, Mike survived a mid-air collision with a tanker near Palomares, Spain, seven months, almost to the hour, after a similar happening to me! A nuclear bomb was lost into the Mediterranean Sea and the hunt for it became one of the important confrontations of the Cold War.

When survival training was complete, our instructors emphasized that we should NOT go out and eat a lot because we were weakened and our stomachs had shrunk. Ha! That morning I ate two large breakfasts and later had a couple of dinners in Harold's Club and the Mapes Hotel. Grabstald, Rooney, and I continued to eat our way across

the country to Kansas where we gorged ourselves throughout three weeks of nuclear weapons training. Then we
snacked our way back to Castle Air Force Base in Central
California for our B-52 checkout before we finally felt satis-
fied. Through all this I never lost or gained a pound. Oh,
for those days once again.

In college, when I studied all night for an exam, I often
got this electric sensation that tingled throughout my body.
Flying long missions in SAC got the feeling going again.
When the body and the mind remain awake for more than
a day, the nerves get tingly, like they are dancing on the
skin's surface. I would often feel this way on long missions
and whenever it did happen, tired as I was, I felt more alive
than at any other time.

The gunner remained awake the entire time we were
north of the Soviet Union. I almost requested him to give
me oxygen checks as I was now beyond tired. I had not
seen the sun for so long that I was confused about time—
even the Aurora began to seem commonplace. I motioned
to Jim, then I disconnected to go downstairs and get a cup
of the worst coffee I've ever tasted—to this day. I had never
been a coffee drinker. Although the coffee was pure caf-
feine, it didn't help. I breathed 100 percent oxygen for a
while. It didn't help either. I wiggled my knees, pinched my
cheeks, and twisted in my seat, anything to try and get the
blood flowing to my brain again. Nothing worked. I was
exhausted.

Pilots have developed a way of flying long distances at

odd hours that gets them some rest. One pilot will doze off and the other will keep an eye on things. Then they switch. Jim noticed that I was maxed out, so he tapped my shoulder and motioned for me to nap for a while. A few seconds later he tapped my shoulder again and the clock said 20 minutes had passed! Time for another fuel log and an oxygen check for the gunner. Outside, the Arctic had not changed, it still looked eerie in the shadow of the earth.

Finally, Terry told us to turn right to something like a heading of north and to prepare to come out of Grid Navigation. It took awhile for that to sink in and then I realized that we were going to head south into Alaska. Man, we had circumnavigated the entire Arctic and had not seen the sun in that time. Headin' south woke us all up for a while.

We descended again to meet another tanker in the Cold Coffee West Refueling Track and picked up another 180,000 pounds of gas. What did that mean? That we could again circumnavigate the Arctic? In the 1950s there were people actually working on a nuclear powered airplane at the Atomic Energy Commission site in the Idaho desert near my hometown. Supposedly, it could stay airborne for weeks but who would they get to fly it? Certainly not me!

Once again we were full of gas and we climbed back up to high altitude. This time we flew clear out of the Aleutian Island chain, all the way to a point off the coast of northern Japan. And then we flew back again to Alaska! By this time my weary brain had forgotten about my weary butt as I swam in a hallucinogenic fog. I thought I had seen the sun rise twice on this mission and was unsure of how many nights I'd lived through—time tricks again, just like at the Stead POW camp. South of Anchorage, we turned for home and were relieved of our nuclear commitment as another of our sister B-52's passed nearby on the same route we had taken the previous day.

After we landed, secured the airplane, and finished both maintenance and intelligence debriefings—I had never in my life been so tired—we loaded our bags into the Air Force blue six-pack truck and headed for the parking lot where some of the wives were waiting to drive their tired husbands home. SAC's wives are a remarkable breed—and that's another story.

Finally, there was only the gunner and me. He was well rested and no longer grouchy, but then, he'd had a couple of nights' sleep during the previous day and a half. He walked over to me with that great, off-centered smile of his and said, "Copilot, let's go get a beer." He flashed those white teeth at me in such a way that I said, "Why not?" I was crazy with fatigue.

Chapter Three

The Cold War often has been analogized as a game of poker. At the table were five powers: the United States, the Soviet Union, Great Britain, France, and China. In 1962, all but China held a nuclear card. However, China was completing work on a nuclear bomb at Lop Nor, a thousand miles north of Mount Everest in the remote Sinkiang Province. France and England, although each possessed a nuclear card, held poor playing hands. Only the United States and the Soviet Union held the strong hands in this most powerful game. And those two were at a nuclear standoff.

In October 1962, the Soviets and Americans laid out onto that poker table everything their societies and cultures had to offer. The bets had been made and there was nothing left to do but stare into each other's eyes and call the hand, or go to war with nuclear weapons. U.S. President John Kennedy and Soviet Premier Nikita Khrushchev symbolically glared at each other, waiting for the other's response. It seems in hindsight that only Kennedy understood what one wrong move might mean.

Americans still do not realize exactly how close they came to nuclear annihilation during the Cuban Missile Crisis of October 1962. It probably was a bit like having a near-miss with an asteroid—we thought a fairly small one had whizzed past the moon and nobody told us otherwise. Only recently did we find out that one of the giants had grazed Earth's atmosphere!

Nuclear war was so close that Khrushchev had already given his commander in Cuba the authority to launch nuclear missiles at U.S. forces, relinquishing his decisional authority over some of his own nuclear weapons. This was unprecedented and it violated the nuclear protocol between our nations! Further, he blatantly cheated by secreting into Cuba an additional 54 tactical nuclear-tipped missiles that Kennedy and the rest of the world did not know about. It was only by a fluke, and Castro's ignorant ego, that they ever were removed.

Krushchev probably was not certifiably crazy, but he surely was close. In 1960, in his address to the United Nations, he took off his shoe and pounded it on the podium, yelling at America that, "We will bury you!" Most Americans nervously laughed off his antics as something "Russian," like it was a strange part of their culture. Actually,

Khrushchev believed in some of his fantasies, sort of like the Caesars of old. He truly thought Russia should rule the world.

So he moved on Cuba—with Castro's delighted encouragement. Khrushchev placed over 40 SS-4 "Sandal" medium range missiles into hard launching sites in Cuba. The Sandal could carry a one-megaton nuclear bomb about 1200 miles. Then he secretly moved an additional 54 short-range "Frog-3" tactical missiles into hidden launching positions throughout the island. The sting for these missiles were a total of 162 nuclear bombs, of which 90 were tactical nukes!

Late in the crisis, Kennedy became aware of only six of the Frog missiles, the other 48 were never discovered! Nor were they, or the tactical nukes, ever accounted for during the Soviet withdrawal because they remained in Cuba, ready to launch, for nearly three months after the crisis had supposedly been settled! Khrushchev's intent was to use them against the United States if we ever attempted another Bay of Pigs. At the height of the crisis, Khrushchev was quoted by an aide saying, "They'd soon realize what a couple of nuclear bursts over New York could do."

In response to U-2 aerial photographs that clearly showed 24 (and later over 40) Sandal missiles being set up in Cuba, Kennedy deployed every available airplane, ship, and missile to the Caribbean Theater and he also readied an invasion force. He raised our DEFense CONdition status to the highest alert in United States history, DEFCON

TWO. DEFCON ONE is considered actual combat with a nuclear exchange already occurring. The Soviets and the Warsaw Pact went to Combat Alert. The U.S. Air Force was sitting Cockpit Alert. All of these forces were loaded with nuclear bombs. Just one spark . . . !

Kennedy's response, as complete as it was, was made without any knowledge of the 54 additional tactical missiles and at least 90 bombs. This was an incredible deception by Khrushchev, who said they were placed there "for the island's defense." He lied, and Kennedy called him a liar (in a diplomatic way, of course) on the last day of the crisis when everything nearly came apart. After Khrushchev agreed to withdraw the missiles and Kennedy agreed not to invade Cuba, a Soviet Surface-to-Air Missile (SAM-2 Guideline) shot down one of our reconnaissance U-2's killing the pilot, Major Rudolph Anderson. This stunned even Khrushchev, because only then did he realize he had lost control of the situation that he, himself, had created.

The world has always thought the end of the Cuban Missile Crisis came when U.S. Secretary of State Dean Rusk said, "We were eyeball to eyeball and the other side just blinked." Rusk saw that Khrushchev realized he'd nearly lost control, nearly cost humanity its world, and with that, Khrushchev backed off the crisis. But he recalled only the Sandal ballistic missiles and six of the Frog tactical missiles that Kennedy knew about, leaving 48 missiles along with 90 tactical nuclear bombs still pointed at the United States from Cuba.

Had there been war, the Soviet's first few tactical nukes would have taken out the U.S. naval fleet in the theater. Next, all our military bases within striking range of Cuba, where many of our forces were waiting to invade, would have disappeared. This preemptive, nuclear first strike by the Soviets, which already had been authorized by Khrushchev, would have necessitated a full-scale nuclear response by the United States. The losses were estimated at up to a half-billion people killed and another half-billion gravely injured. Much of the rest of the world probably would have slowly starved, frozen, or died an agonizing death from radiation fallout and nuclear winter.

Unbelievably, we did not have a hot line for communication between our countries at the time, so Khrushchev agreed to terms by announcing the agreement over Moscow radio to the Russian people—who had not been told there was a crisis. Our embassy picked up the message, as intended, and immediately forwarded the news to Kennedy. What a way to run a war! Just one more move and the world, as we knew it, would have ended.

Castro was furious throughout the crisis. He was neither consulted nor was he informed of anything and he felt like the pawn that he truly was. Castro knew about the 48 missiles with their accompanying tactical nuclear bombs that remained in Cuba. He wrote a letter to Khrushchev suggesting, in a "nice" way, to launch them at the United States but Khrushchev had already backed off. Then Castro stupidly told his people at the United Nations that he still possessed the 48 missiles and their nuclear warheads. That's when Khrushchev blew up at Castro and pulled out all of them. This was in January 1963, nearly three months after the crisis supposedly ended! Castro could have taken control of those nukes at any time and by launching only one, well . . . you get the picture. Now, maybe the world can begin to understand why the United States is waiting for Castro to die and why we have not invaded Cuba since that time. We will maintain our embargo . . . probably.

Just because one of the superpowers had backed off the Cuban thing didn't mean the shooting was over. The next phase of the Cold War got hot. The Soviet Union had been deeply humiliated and they resented having to remove their missiles in front of the eyes of the world. They also had to find a new place to export what the rest of the world did not want, their brand of the "dictatorship of the proletariat"—world communism. After Cuba, Americans especially would have none of that mischief. Of course, we did have our leftists but at the time they were considered quirky by most people.

When the missiles of October were gone, a couple of years went by before Khrushchev was quietly removed from office and placed into a luxurious dacha outside Moscow. Soon though, he was taken to a small hut to live out his life in intended obscurity. When he died, not a single Communist official went to pay last respects. To them, Khrushchev had become a "non-person."

Leonid Brezhnev became Premier of the Soviets. He

was a man of quiet, incarnate evil, but he was not out-landish like Khrushchev. As an old, hard-line Stalinist, he maintained total control and, like Stalin, it is unknown exactly how many people he sent to the Gulag. Brezhnev, however, was a realist. He knew the United States would totally destroy the Soviet Union if he tossed even one nuke our way. This policy, adopted by both sides, was called "Mutually Assured Destruction." That it was! The acronym was MAD. Both superpowers remained in this nuclear standoff mode for a number of decades after the Cuban Missile Crisis ended. It was something we'd all been used to for far too long.

During this era, China entered the throes of a cultural revolution. They devised "five-year plans" and "great leaps forward" and forced their people to be enthusiastic in their acceptance of some really crazy communist ideas. China's supreme dictator, Mao Tse Tung, probably was well inten-tioned, but just one of those great leaps forward created a famine throughout China from 1958 to 1961. It killed an estimated 40 million people. Mao also was directly respon-sible for the executions of another 45 million Chinese as a matter of Communist policy. These "verified estimates" are most likely on the low side, but it still adds up to 85 million people killed in China alone just to maintain an incredibly flawed and totalitarian political system.

Although her strength always lay in her population, by now nearing a billion people, China removed herself from becoming a potential superpower for generations. Our soldiers in Korea remember well the seemingly endless wave of padded-vest Chinese that invaded across the Yalu River that terribly cold winter in January 1951. It didn't seem to bother Mao that he might get nuked. He felt China would be far better off with fewer people anyway. He was a chillingly cold-blooded killer.

In 1979 China instituted a program whereby each Chinese family could have only one child. Huge fines prevented more than one birth per family and so, many infants were killed. This program is still in place in China and there is a shortage of women (feminists note) because the Chinese, if they can have only one child, want sons. Well, guess what happened to a lot of baby girls.

From World War II through the Korean War and Vietnam, the buildup of armed forces was the main expense for both superpowers. Each side came out of World War II with certain strengths and weaknesses but the Soviet Union kept its society closed off from the rest of the world with what Winston Churchill described as an "Iron Curtain." Many people died just trying to cross it. I've seen it and it was the bleakest place I've ever been. Mile-wide, plowed, and mined fields, guard towers, patrol dogs, stern, unsmiling faces, machine gun emplacements—all designed to keep people inside communism's bleak world.

The Soviets had a lot of catching up to do for a very good reason. In 1937, prior to Russia's entry into World War II, Stalin began a purge of his military and executed almost all of his senior military leadership. In his paranoia, he also executed over half of his officer corps, which caused him grave problems throughout World War II. Beyond that, unbelievably, he also purged over one third of the members of his own Communist party. The murder of 13-million people—all this just to prove loyalty to his leadership! And that was only one of his numerous purges. Russia lost over 30 million people in World War II, far more than ALL the other combatant nations combined, including the deaths of most European Jews. Get this: It is estimated that Stalin killed many more of his own people than Russia lost in that war!

In the autumn of 1942, with most of the Soviet military leadership already buried, the Nazis easily advanced to the gates of Moscow and they captured much of Stalingrad. It was largely through the heroic efforts of the Russian people, and the few good generals who had not been purged, that the Nazi's were defeated. The frightful Russian winter, that also got Napoleon, sealed the German Army's fate. Hitler abandoned them. Very few ever came home. About 250,000 Germans fought at Stalingrad. Over 140,000 were killed, the rest surrendered, were taken to the Gulag, and, long after World War II ended, less than 5,000 came home.

Being a supreme dictator, "political leadership" was Stalin's strong suit, and this saddled the military leaders and thinkers who survived his purges with communist "polit-think." To Stalin, Free World political leaders were weak because they had to be elected every few years and, in that way, a democracy must reinvent the wheel each time a new leader was elected. Khrushchev considered Kennedy flawed because he came from wealthy, soft stock and not the peasantry, like himself. It is an understatement to say the Soviets did not understand that our machinery was already in place through our constitution and that most of the Free World was adopting democracy and economic capitalism.

The Soviet people lived for most of the twentieth century in a secret society, much like those of us in the Strategic Air Command. The difference between SAC and the U.S.S.R. was that SAC briefed us on everything that went on in the world, whereas the peoples of the communist countries were informed of only whatever their governments wanted them to believe.

For decades the Soviet Union stole U.S. technology, including the atomic bomb, and they used it to build an armed force that appeared equal to our own. As soon as a new weapons system was developed in the United States, one exactly like it showed up in Moscow's arsenal. They used captured German scientists from World War II to leap ahead of us in missile technology and in such obscure but vital areas as orbital mechanics, the mathematics of missiles and satellites.

Under Brezhnev, the Soviet Union still wanted to control the world, and it exported instability everywhere. But they found that Africa was virtually impenetrable, and Latin America too close to the United States and too far from the Soviet Union to give it area more than a token try. Cuba had been a disaster for them. Korea had been a stalemate. India was friendly but too disorganized, and it had only recently been freed from Britain's colonialism. The Arab states could neither be controlled nor could they be trusted to incubate communism. The First World, the free, industrialized states that practiced capitalism, would have none of their communist shenanigans. So where?

Communism was already established, though still in its adolescence, in southeast Asia. By 1963, the French colony of Vietnam, which had been smoldering since World War II, was ready to flame. Vietnam had been occupied by the Japanese but after the Allied victory, France insisted upon regaining its old colony. Ho Chi Minh asked the United States for help but, because we were aligned with France during the big war, we were politically forced to let them re-colonize Vietnam. An angry Ho then went to Moscow for help and got it!

With this Soviet help, Ho Chi Minh, and his very able General Vo Nguyen Giap, soundly defeated the arrogant French in April and May 1954, in a remote valley of western North Vietnam at a place called Dien Bien Phu. There, roughly 8,000 French soldiers and foreign legionnaires were killed by the continuous pounding of General Giap's artillery. The remainder of the French garrison, 10,000 men, was marched toward Hanoi, but only half lived through the 60-day march. The weak were left by the roadside—or shot, like our own soldiers, sailors, and marines were during the infamous Bataan Death March of World War II. Of the 5,000 that reached Hanoi, less than 2,500 survived. No one knows for certain how many (or how few) of these men lived to tell their grandchildren about their adventures. For years France tried to buy back some of these old prisoners of War for roughly one million dollars each but, like the Germans abandoned in Russia, only a few ever returned. This, while American POW's were also incarcerated! Where was the French outrage? For that matter, where was our own?

After Dien Bien Phu, the 1954 Geneva Convention split Vietnam into two countries at the 17th Parallel and created a distance of 20 miles between them as a Demilitarized Zone, which later became famous as the DMZ. Roughly 20 million people lived in each country, and they were given about a year to choose which side they wanted to live in. Over two million people crossed to the south to enjoy what they thought was going to be freedom. Almost none moved north except for those hard-core Communists who went there to train as Viet Cong. At the time they were known as Viet Minh and they were fanatic about regaining South Vietnam for themselves.

It is an unfortunate fact of human nature that one man has always wanted to rule another. Of course, this has led to fighting, wars, pestilence, famine . . . if only mankind could control this urge. But no, we always have had and always will have wars and rumors of wars because of this element in human nature. Some must fight if others are to live. This rule led to the development of newer weapons from the spear and the sword to the Roman catapult, to the longbow, the gun, the rifle, the cannon, the tank, the airplane, the jet bomber, the rocket . . . the nuclear bomb. Along with weapons development came all the other technologies that have allowed man to gradually better his lot. This may be unfortunate, but it is fact: man could not have landed upon the moon had not he first developed the rocket, and all before it—for war.

The two nuclear superpowers kept their distance from each other for another 30 years. Peace was maintained by an alert America using the Triad, her nuclear defense/offense consisting of Polaris, Poseidon, and Trident nuclear submarines, Titan and Minuteman intercontinental ballistic missiles (ICBM's), and the B-52.

Three men were instrumental in building the Triad for America. Admiral Hyman Rickover almost single-handedly developed the nuclear submarine for the U.S. Navy. Wernher Von Braun, who saved himself from becoming a Russian by crossing a wartime Germany and surrendering to the Americans, built and tested U.S. rockets for moon shots and for the ICBM's we aimed at the Soviet Union and China. The third leg of the Triad was our bomber force, which was developed by Air Force General Curtis E. LeMay.

All of these submarines, rockets, and bombers cost huge sums of money to build and maintain. For decades the United States spent up to eight percent of its gross national product on the Triad as a nuclear deterrence. It was incredibly expensive but it would have cost us our civilization had we dropped our shield and let the Soviets have their way. They were entirely serious about "burying us" as Khrushchev was fond of saying.

In 1947, Congress authorized the restructuring of the U.S. military and the Air Force was born from the U.S. Army Air Corps. It quickly became a bomber command, to the consternation of America's fighter jocks, and General LeMay constructed the most powerful armed force ever known, calling it the Strategic Air Command. By 1962 Boeing had built 742 of the giant B-52's. All were kept flying or in any of several stages of alert, always ready to go to war in case the communists tried a nuclear first strike at America or her allies. Clearly and justifiably, the United States did not trust the communists.

LeMay was famous for having a cigar stuck in his mouth most of the time. Once, when he was boarding one of his planes, an aide said, "Sir, could you please put out that cigar? The plane might blow up!" LeMay glared at the aide and replied, "It wouldn't dare!" And that became his trademark. He was no nonsense, as a generation of Air Force men found out. In World War II he was the commanding general of the Twenty First (XXI) Bomber Command, which dropped the atomic bombs on Japan to end that war. He had no compunction about dropping nukes on America's enemies if it came to that, and he trained his men to think the same way. And we did!

LeMay's men came from all walks of American life and they were smart, dedicated, and hard-working. They knew how serious the Cold War had become, it was no secret. A military draft was in place and every able-bodied young man in America was required to serve a minimum of three years on active military duty—remember? Usually they got drafted into the Army. Because of that draft, the Air Force and Navy were able to attract some of America's best and brightest young men. The lure of high technology, hands-on experience, and a grand sense of adventure attracted many.

Tom Brokaw called Americans who fought World War II the "Greatest Generation," and the country has accepted this as fact. They were truly great, and they saved our society, but who were they? They had won a world war on two fronts and immediately afterward faded into obscurity. Some of them may have lived next door or even in the same house, yet few of us knew exactly who they were because almost every man from that war, although a hero, chose not to glorify himself. These guys did not want to relive their war, they wanted to build houses and raise families. They came home and did just that, quietly building a newer, even better nation—and the results of their actions exceeded everyone's economic expectations. Many experienced veterans of World War II remained in the military, for one reason or another, and it was this core of experienced military men who led America through the Cold War.

Combat experience is a rare and exceptionally valuable thing. Throughout history, green recruits fail unless

they have been given intelligent and realistic combat training before they actually enter the arena. Combat veterans,
should they live so long and if you can get them to do it,
will pass along stories of their experiences, usually in the
form of "war stories and other lies."

The 320th Bomb Wing, and in particular its 441st Bomb
Squadron, had combat veterans in abundance. The alert
pad at Mather was populated with these old-head World
War II pilots and radar navigators. I was vaguely aware that
most of the older men flew in the "Rilly Big War" but none
of them ever talked about it and we younger guys felt like
fools even thinking about marching up to ask, "Did you
rilly fly in the rilly big one?" We might have been given an
answer, "Why yes, Son, I really did." If they talked about
anything it was about current life in SAC.

I finished reading a book one day on the alert pad and
told Bill Hart about it. Immediately he was interested in the
story line. He read the book and it changed his personal-
ity for the rest of the alert tour. The book was about him!
It was a fictionalized account of a B-52 that flew a Chrome
Dome mission where the cockpit heat went to full hot.
There was no substitute B-52 that could take their mission,
and so they suffered a debilitating, high temperature in the
cockpit, trying everything to shut the recalcitrant valve.
Returning to Mather after descending to below 10,000 feet
to depressurize and cool off the forward cockpit, they were
too woozy with heat exhaustion to realize the B-52 ate fuel
like a monster at low altitude. They ran out of gas just short

of Beale AFB, California, and bailed out low to the ground. The plane crashed but did not burn (no fuel) and some huge nuclear bombs survived undamaged. Wow! Lucky or what?

This was a story Bill Hart was only willing to discuss after somebody had written a barefaced novel about him and the others on his crew. What Bill never discussed was his work in the air over Europe. There must have been 20 or 30 other men I lived, worked, and flew with who had flown the B-17's, B-24's, and B-29's over Europe and Japan, and none of them talked about anything. These guys were my childhood heroes! As a child, I had logged many hours flying over Europe with them, raiding with Doolittle or going against Japanese fighters with the Flying Tigers. I will single out only a few guys to discuss here, knowing they all had their stories.

Our wing commander, Colonel Van R. Parker, was one of these World War II greats. He was a big man who exuded confidence and leadership and, from the back of the alert pad briefing room, he looked almost exactly like John Wayne! Same squinty-eyed smile, same self-assurance, same poise, and he never asked or ordered us to do anything he would not do right along with us or that he already had not done a hundred times himself. He was one of those rare men whose combat experience was exceptionally valuable to America.

Few people knew Colonel Parker's story but I've read his fine book, *Dear Folks,* where I found out that he actually was commissioned into the US Army Cavalry—as a horse soldier! Whooda thunk it? John Wayne as a horse soldier? It gets a lot better because the Army abandoned the Cavalry soon after and the young Lieutenant Parker got himself assigned to airplanes. Part of his problem was that he was a really good pilot, so the Army Air Corps kept him home from the early part of World War II and had him teach others how to fly. This gnawed at his craw until he got to fly the newest bomber out of Boeing's plant, the B-29.

He lived in the room next to Jimmy Stewart, the movie star, while they checked out together in bombers at Gowan Field in Boise, Idaho. Eventually, Major Stewart was reassigned to fly B-24's in Europe where he flew a full combat tour. How many people knew that? Growing up, I thought he played trombone and led the Glenn Miller Orchestra during that war. Jimmy Stewart eventually rose to the rank of Brigadier General in the Air Force Reserves.

Captain Parker was reassigned to Guam with the first B-29 combat contingent of World War II. On his first mission he flew near enough to Iwo Jima to look down and see one of the bloodiest battles in history being fought right before his eyes. After 31 horrifying missions over Japan, losing many of his good friends, the war finally ended with the atomic bombings of Hiroshima and Nagasaki. Parker had landed twice upon Iwo Jima, once with battle damage, while the fight for that speck of an island was still raging! The volcanic Iwo Jima was littered with B-29 carcasses and otherwise filled with neat rows of white crosses. There was not one tree on the island. It smelled of death.

When the war was over and the Japanese leaders boarded the USS *Missouri* to sign their surrender in front of General MacArthur, it was the young Major Parker who led the squadron of B-29's over the battleship *Missouri* and Tokyo Bay as an American show of force. An exceptional honor—and he barely mentioned it in his book!

In the secret little world in which a few generals select those captains and majors who will rise in rank to the highest level, it was obvious that Colonel Parker, would have, earlier, been one of those selected. Eventually, he would have become commander of Strategic Air Command but, as events unfolded that will be seen as the thrust of this book, he was taken off the list.

There were many other heroes at Mather that I did not know about. Our squadron commander was Lieutenant Colonel Ralph W. Jones, and what a combat history he has! If someone stuck a top hat on his head, plastered a beard upon his face, then dressed him in a black long coat of the mid-nineteenth Century, he would be indistinguishable from Abraham Lincoln himself, including the large ears. I came to admire this man like I have always admired the real Abe Lincoln.

I've watched the movie *Twelve O'Clock High* so many times that I know the script by heart. It is based upon pure fact, as was another World War II flying movie, *Memphis Belle*. The *Belle* was the first B-17 to survive 25 missions over Europe in World War II. One of the first pilots to survive 25 missions in a B-17 in the European Theater was none other than Colonel Jones, who was one of only four young pilots in his group even to survive! He and a friend have a friendly argument going as to which of them was the first American pilot ever to fly a B-17 into Germany.

Further, the movie *Twelve O'Clock High* was written about his group, the 306th, which was multiplied by three to get the fictional 918th Group for the movie. In the 8th Air Force, to become one of only four pilots to survive out of a whole group was like winning the lottery. Do we remember that over ten percent of all Americans killed in World War II were lost while flying bombers over Europe? More Americans died in those bombers than all the Marines we lost throughout the Pacific War!

Colonel Jones was my first squadron commander and, although I've worked for many super guys in a long career, there were very few as fine as this man. He was fair, worked about 25 hours each day, and could get his men to do things they might not otherwise have done—like work 80- to 100-hour weeks! Somehow, he kept about 150 guys, each with ideas of his own, headed in the right direction. I would liken it to herding cats!

Colonel Jones had a henchman called Colonel Kline to help him herd us cats. My nemesis! Colonel Kline supervised the operations of our squadron. I was never certain if he was truly mean or just acted gruff for effect, but he had me scared to death for my entire B-52 career. Long after we had all retired I saw him again at a reunion and called him "Colonel Kline" like I had always done. He glared at me and ordered me to call him "Jim," but he was smiling. Yes, he still scared me, and yet, he was a wonderful guy with a great sense of humor. And he made a fine henchman.

Another man I became very close with, and who is still considered part of my family, is Lieutenant Colonel Charles P. Andermann. As a second lieutenant navigator in World War II, Chuck was shot down in a B-17 over Austria and captured by the Nazi's. He spent the remainder of the war in Stalag Luft III with the men who made "The Great Escape." After the war he stayed on in the Air Force and was thinking of retirement when I met him on alert in late 1964. Later, he became my radar navigator and, on our second combat tour, we flew 30 combat missions together in the B-52.

I would be remiss if I did not mention the gunners who also roamed our alert pad. The B-52 carried only one gunner in the tail. The B-17 had five gunners: two in the waist, a tail gunner, a top turret gunner, and, of course, the ball turret gunner. The ball turret was such a tiny place that they chose recruits for their small size and trained them to squeeze into the ball turret, only later expecting them to fire a gun. I've had good reason to bitch about my size, short and skinny (now I gripe the other way on the latter), and had I lived during the Second World War, that's what they would have made me do, be a ball turret gunner! No thanks! It was arguably the most dangerous job in that war. Besides, I'd rather fly the airplane.

Like the rest of our aircrews, the gunners had two age groups. The old head gunners at Mather were the very ones who fired those waist, tail and turret guns during the "Big Conflict." They suffered a very high loss rate, and I'm certain none of them will ever forget their days flying combat. Nobody ever does. The younger gunners were just like us new guy pilots and navs, they were sort of in awe about their childhood heroes too.

There was a little war heating up in South East Asia and none of us paid any attention to it until the Viet Cong attacked a U.S.Army camp at Pleiku in the Central Highlands of South Vietnam. They killed 27 American Special Forces advisors! This attack, far more than the Gulf of Tonkin incident several months earlier, affected the lives of all Americans because it was the falling leaf that tickled the nose of and awakened a slumbering giant who got really pissed off that somebody was killing her soldiers. Americans, if they remember correctly, demanded a strong response to the Pleiku attack, and this was when our commitment to Vietnam began in earnest.

Chapter Four

When I was a little kid most of my friends and cousins wanted to grow up to become cowboys, which seemed to be an honorable profession for boys out West. Pocatello, Idaho, was a small railroad town with a small college and a Class C professional baseball team called the Cardinals. Except for those damn Yankee fans, everyone's hero was Stan Musial, a St. Louis Cardinal. By the time I was six I had developed three childhood dreams about what I wanted to do with my life. Should I become Roy Rogers, or Stan Musial, or should I fly airplanes? From the time I saw my first jet, I never wavered from my goal of the third option, but there were temptations.

I was born to war, just before World War II, and did not know there was such a thing as peace until I was age five. The war did affect us what with rationing, the shortages, the warplanes that trained at our nearby airfield, the soldiers and sailors passing through the railroad depot on their way to the Pacific War. We never saw the wounded but, nonetheless, we kids sensed the seriousness of the situation.

After the war ended, my parents took me to an airshow where I heard a jet fly overhead. I couldn't see it because I was so small and the crowd was large and tightly packed. But I knew that jet I'd heard went really fast! Dad lifted me up onto his shoulders, and still, I could not see the jet because the sound followed behind the plane and that's where my young eyes searched. The magic of that one moment affected me far more than the war.

When we got home I told Dad that I was going to become a jet pilot and I meant it! He did not laugh but he sat me down and told me I could not fly jets because they went so fast the human mind could not keep up with their speed. Later, I found out he was correct, that jet pilots needed to think far ahead of what was happening. But his words did not deter me. From that moment forward, whatever turns my life took, I was going to fly jets and that was that. No more Roy Rogers. No more Stan Musial.

I had a children's book about a boy who sat in a box with a stick and pretended he was flying. Boxes were available and sticks were plentiful, and I flew a few good missions until the boxes broke or got wet in the rain. These flights of fantasy set me free. Sometime later I decided to become an astronaut, long before the term "astronaut" was coined, before most people knew that rockets could put things into orbit. I fantasized about the first manned mission to Mars! But I had a lot of growing up to do before I would be old enough to do these things, so I set aside my dreams and waited to grow up.

Probably the most important influence upon my young life was my maternal grandfather, a tall, balding, potbellied man everyone called "Pop." He used to slip me nickels for things a small boy might need and I learned the value of money by spending those nickels. A candy bar was a nickel and so was an ice cream cone. It seemed everything cost a nickel. Throughout my life I've been really cheap because of this feeling that everything should cost a nickel.

I often got to spend the weekend with Pop until he moved in with us permanently. We were pals and we slept together. It was like sleeping on the side of a mountain, and I learned to hang my leg over my side of the bed just to hold on. He read dime "whodunits" every night and we listened to all the Pocatello Cardinal games together. Sometimes he took me to the ballpark for the real thing and he would slip me a dime to pay for my own ticket. With Pop around, my life was generally idyllic.

He created dreams of wanderlust in my young mind, telling me stories of his own youth about how he grew up in a small town in Indiana where the kids tied ropes around tree limbs and swung out into the river to drop with gleeful splashes in cannonball dives. They fished, explored, and had secret caves to keep their booty hidden, especially from girls.

Pop loved baseball and eventually played catcher for the Cincinnati Red Stockings. He was called "Red" Boyatt then, for his Irish red hair, and he was a smart catcher. He taught me that the catcher actually controlled the game, like a football quarterback, explaining that he was the only player who could see the entire field. But being a catcher had its drawbacks as his fingers were masses of large, broken knuckles where the fast balls had all but destroyed them in the days before good catcher's mitts.

I'll never forget one of Pop's stories. Cincinnati was playing in Chicago. My clever grandfather peeled a potato into the shape of a baseball and when it dried out it turned a greenish black, the same color as a well-used, grass-stained baseball of the era. He said baseballs were scarce back then and they were used until sometimes you could knock the cover off with a solid hit. It doesn't happen today, as baseballs are replaced after even a minor scruff, but a hundred years ago there were some loose rules to go along with the loose covers in the game of baseball.

Bottom of the ninth, Chicago was trailing Cincinnati by a run. They had men on first and second with two out and a guy like "Casey" stepped up to the plate. Red watched the eyes of the man on second and studied the elementary signals passed to the batter and the runners. He knew Chicago needed to get both base runners into scoring position and he understood what their eyes were saying. He called for a fast pitch outside—and the runners broke! He pulled the potato out from behind his catcher's vest and hurled it over the third baseman, far into left field. Both runners tore for another extra base. Red turned around and showed the umpire the baseball in his mitt and said, "That was a potato, this is the baseball!" He tagged the runner out, the game was over and he got, "run outta town on a rail." It was the first time I ever heard the term "tarred and feathered." He never again played in Chicago. The rules of baseball were changed but some minor league catcher tried the same trick in the 1970s. It was disallowed because there was this ancient rule applied to baseball because of my grandfather.

Pop joined the Army in time for the Spanish American War. When he returned home he met and married my grandmother, "Mom." She was about half his size and this doomed me to genetic impairment because three of my four grandparents were about five feet tall! With a newfound responsibility Pop needed a job so he joined the carnival, saying he could play the trombone when he could not! But he learned quickly. The carnival traveled throughout the West and finally went broke in Pocatello. They had to stay!

My aunt and uncle had a dry farm in the North Gem Valley of rural Idaho where I spent most of my summers until age twelve. We did not know we were poor. We drew water from a well, milked cows, raised chickens, slopped pigs, and did our duties in an old outhouse. When the eggs were gathered and the other chores, mostly concerning the animals, were finished, I played baseball with my two cousins, Jay Mack and Ben.

There was a corral where a pile of dried horse manure served as our backstop. Jay Mack was the New York Yankees. I've never been a Yankees fan because Ben and I were the Cleveland Indians, who always came in second to the Yankees except in 1948. I wanted to be the Cardinals but they outvoted me and besides, they said, it was their pile of horse manure! Jay Mack always won our games because he was a couple of years older than Ben and me, was an athlete of exceptional ability, and was a very good pitcher. He was also the umpire. On top of that, he could beat up the both of us whenever he wanted. We played with rocks and an old tree limb until Pop saw us one day and decided that we should try the game with real bats and balls. After that he kept us supplied.

When we weren't doing chores or playing baseball, we were exploring. My Aunt Marge made us jam sandwiches, with home-churned butter on homemade bread. She wrapped them in wax paper and put them, along with crackers and a jar of fresh milk, into a paper sack for us. Then we were off to explore and play little Indian boys who did a lot of hunting around the farm with imaginary bows and arrows.

The farm had been a stopover on the old Oregon Trail and there was a spring of fresh water where the pioneers built a rock watering trough against a lava outcrop. One day Ben and I noticed a hornets' nest on the lava above the trough. Of course, we had to throw rocks at the thing and, finally, one of us hit it. We then learned how mad a hornet could get. We ran as fast as we could but it was not fast enough. An old log outbuilding was the only refuge around and, as we ran toward it, I tripped and fell flat onto a low-lying cactus. Ben ran past me and made it to the outbuilding, the hornets flying over me to get to Ben—and he got stung several times. I didn't suffer any stings, but I've always wondered who got the worst of the deal, as I looked like a porcupine with all those cactus spines sticking out of me.

Occasionally, we got into trouble and got "lickin's" which hurt but kept us straight. When I was about eight, on my first night at the farm for the summer, we were all excited and carrying on in the upstairs bedroom. I felt special to get to sleep between Jay Mack and Ben and we giggled a lot. All of a sudden, on some signal between them, they both raised the covers above my head and pinned them around me. Then they farted. Of course this caused a great commotion and soon my Uncle Lawrence was at the foot of the stairs hollering, "j-MAAAACK . . . you boys go to sleep. Now!" His voice struck terror into our hearts and we quieted down for a while.

Then they did it again! Same commotion. But this time Lawrence called us downstairs for what we thought was going to be a good lickin.' No such luck. He led us outside in our underwear and told Jay Mack to climb up on the old log barn and sleep on the split-rail roof. Jay hustled up, threw his leg over the crest, and went promptly to sleep. Lawrence then took me to the chicken coop, swept a couple of hens off their roost, and set me on the highest roost. How indignant! I was humiliated. So were the chickens. They crooked their heads and looked at me with real funny expressions for a while. I guess they figured I was a really weird chicken.

Lawrence saved the best for Ben. Just before I arrived for the summer, he had dug a new "toilet hole" for the outhouse, and he was waiting for some farmer friends to come over and help him move it. Four men took a couple two-by-fours to lift and carry it about ten feet to the new hole. Then they threw the freshly dug dirt into the old hole. That's how people lived before flush toilets. Yes, the Sears catalogue came in right handy.

The new toilet hole was just a big hole in the ground about five feet deep, and that's where Ben was dropped. And I thought I was indignant! Ben found a sprig of sagebrush, and began to scrape out climbing holds in one corner. He finally got a few hand and footholds made, and then he climbed out. When he got his head above ground level, there was his dad in all his midnight terror! Lawrence simply said, "Boo!" And Ben fell back into the hole where he stayed for a while longer.

Meantime, I climbed down off the roost to look out the window of the chicken coop to see whatever I could see, when suddenly, the door of the coop flew open and there, silhouetted in the light of a full moon, stood my Uncle Lawrence! Reaction was quick and I began bawling, "I fell off the roost! I fell off the roost!" There was no sympathy. He scraped a few more chickens off their sleeping quarters and, again, placed me on that damned roost. I wished I had gotten the barn. Jay Mack was still asleep.

A few minutes later Lawrence gathered us up and herded us back to bed. I guess we were supposed to learn something, but I don't know what. We did go straight to sleep, however. This story has been banging around our family for decades and at Thanksgiving reunions we still get a chuckle—with my uncle chuckling the deepest.

When I was ten, I got to stay for a few weeks in the small town of Arco with my other cousins, Sally and Julie. There wasn't much to do in Arco except to play baseball—with girls. In June 1950, a short time before the North Koreans invaded South Korea to begin the Korean War, a small article in the newspaper (I was looking for baseball scores) caught my eye. The article also intrigued Sally.

The Atomic Energy Commission (AEC), which built all of America's nuclear reactors at their site near Arco, was going to use their Experimental Breeder Reactor Number One (EBR-1) to make electricity for Arco. The news article said that this was to be the world's first commercial use of nuclear power, a significant historical event. History meant nothing to us kids but we thought it might be fun. There was not another soul in this small town of about 400 people who was interested in this event. Most of the adults would be either in church or down at the bar and all of the kids would be out playing hide and seek.

The news article said the AEC would change over to nuclear power at exactly eight o'clock that night. And so Sally and I turned off all the lights except for one hall light near the bedrooms. We hid behind the piano in the living room and peeked around the corner, hoping to see a small fireball and a mushroom cloud erupt from that single light bulb.

Eight o'clock arrived, and nothing happened. The light bulb didn't even flicker. After about five minutes Sally got up enough nerve to step into the hallway and turn the light off and on several times. Nothing happened except that the light went on and off like it was supposed to. Oh well. We went back outside to play, and the next day we were surprised to see another article in the paper that said the experiment had been a huge success. We didn't see how it possibly could have been a success because nothing happened! There was no mushroom cloud!

Years later we both realized that we were probably the only people who weren't involved with the experiment, to have witnessed the first peaceful, commercial use of nuclear energy in the history of the world. Everyone else in Arco was not interested. Someday, the power of the atom will drive the world economy, and Sally and I were right there to witness absolutely nothing when it first happened. EBR-1 is now a National Monument.

The friends I grew up with are still close to my heart although we went our separate ways. My first friends were in my Sunday School class at church. When we got old enough, we would meet at Sunday School and then skip church afterward to play baseball or football in the park across the street. One winter Sunday the snow was deep outside so we got a roll of toilet paper and played football in the church basement—during services!

The crashing of tables and chairs and the hooting glee of about eight boys disrupted the services and, shortly, we were staring at the minister, several elders, and my dad, who was Sunday School Superintendent. They halted services to deal with a problem they'd had for years, unruly, unrepentant boys. Dad said all of us would probably wind up in prison, that we would never get anywhere in life. I'm sure it upset him later to learn that all of us became quite successful, largely because of the ethics we learned in Sunday School. With us the process had to be pure osmosis. Thankfully, they didn't have drugs like Ritalin in those days, or we'd all have become zombies!

They tried to make us into little deacons and tried to get us to sing in the church choir. To this day I'll be happy to admit that I cannot sing. I can bellow off-key, but sing? The choir let me go when they realized this fact.

There was always live music in our house. I grew up with Mozart, Hayden, Brahms, Beethoven, a lot of Bach, Tchaikovsky, Chopin, and Williams—Roger Williams. For years we did not have a phonograph, and stereos had not yet been invented, but we've always had a piano. Mom played the piano several hours each day and I got to a point where I "felt" the compositions even more than just hearing them. She was good, more than good, and I loved listening to her play. Roger Williams, who was known as Louie Wertz before he became famous, went to our church. He studied with the same piano teacher who taught my three younger sisters until he moved to New York and recorded "Autumn Leaves."

It was kind of nice growing up in a house with so much music until my sisters began their piano lessons. Can you imagine, for a moment, what it was like having to listen to all those one-hand scale exercises? Or very simple melodies that would not leave your head until the baseball game started? Rhythms that were broken to mend mistakes? Whole compositions played, not for pleasure or listening enjoyment, but rather to repeat a passage, ineptly, over and over, with no interpretation of the music itself? It drove me completely nuts. When one sister finally got good enough to tolerate, the next one began her lessons, and then the next. This was not music! This was madness! During this era of my life, I learned to live outdoors and I played a lot of baseball. Summers were wonderful because I could escape to the farm.

Three sisters practicing their music was as horrible as any hell I was taught to endure in case of capture by the communists. To this very day, hell, to me, is not fire and brimstone, it's listening to some kid practicing scales. I successfully escaped music, through baseball, until I was in the seventh grade. Dad tried to stick a trumpet into my mouth and all he got for his effort was spit in his trumpet. I couldn't blow one clean note. Mom made me take three piano lessons before I got wise and did not show up, and said, "I forgot." She knew better.

Mom played piano for the Kasai Dance Studio to pay for my three sisters' dance lessons. She made me attend a few sessions where I was forced—mind you, forced—to learn how to waltz. And with a girl! For crying out loud, no self-respecting seventh grader should know how to waltz! It was the only dance I ever learned, however, because I rarely got to dance after my freshman year in high school. Instead, I was given a drum. It is the only thing I still have from my childhood.

My parents have always been first-class musicians, Dad on the trumpet and Mom on the piano. During his high school years, Dad played in a trumpet trio which took first place in the national music festival in Evanston, Illinois. He's age 86 now and still plays Taps for the funerals of most of Pocatello's veterans. Mom has been the church organist for over 60 years. When I'm home they still wrangle me into playing with them for dances at the old folks' center, something I thoroughly enjoy.

Pocatello is a Mormon community, and it must have been the dancing center of the world. Mormons love to dance, and it infected everyone else. When they were both in college, Dad was playing for a Mormon dance and spotted Mom dancing. In mid-tune, he leaped off the stage and cut in. Apparently, it worked, and I was born a few years later. Every Friday and Saturday night of my youth, Mom and Dad were gone playing for dances.

In high school my buddies and I discovered an interest in girls, and the only place to meet them was at Mormon dances. We pretended to be good Mormon kids in order to get into the Stake House where they held dances for teens on Saturday nights. We usually stood around gawking at the girls and wishing we had the nerve to ask one to dance, along with the ability to move her properly around the floor. The band did not play many waltzes, but when they did, I would bundle up my nerves and head toward the girl of my dreams. Two things usually happened at this point: one, she'd get asked to dance by another guy just before I got there, or two, I'd chicken out! But it was still fun to stand around with my friends.

Halloween of my freshman year in high school, Dad came home complaining that his drummer was drunk again. I had the misfortune of being there when he got home, and I could see the light that seemed to come on behind his eyes. He'd always said that it didn't take any brains to be a drummer. In fact, I've heard him say a hundred times, "A drummer is just a musician with his brains knocked out!" He might have been joking, sort of, but it confirmed what I already knew: I was NOT a musician. However, I could see what Dad was thinking, and I didn't scoot out the back door in time. He figured I would become his new drummer!

"We're going down to Ford Music right now and I'm going to buy you a drum set," he declared. We bought the drum set, I financed it and he cosigned for me, and I've been in debt from that day on. In our living room that afternoon, Dad showed me all he knew about playing the drums for a dance. The lesson lasted only a few minutes. It was "Boom, chunk, Boom, chunk." Right foot on the bass drum pedal, left foot on the high hat cymbals. "Boom, chunk, Boom, chunk." Three hours later I was doing this in front of all my friends at the Stake House dance!

My first dance job! And I was supposed to be down with my buddies gawking at girls. Instead, I was on the bandstand, completely destroying anybody's idea of dancing. It was truly terrible. I played, "Boom, chunk," a lot, just like Dad showed me. We played a couple of waltzes, and then I played, "Boom, chunk, chunk. Boom, chunk, chunk." Mom buried her humiliation behind her piano, and Dad suffered out front—and it served him right. As for me, I was fairly oblivious to what was going on except for my buddies pointing and giggling. The saxophone player was a good Mormon fellow, but I think he took up drinking after that dance.

My parents never again played at the Stake House, and it was many years before I played there again. Eventually, I got a bit better. Around my eighteenth birthday, I got to "sit in" with Louis Armstrong. That, to this day, is still one of my happiest and proudest moments, but I was going to fly jets, and nothing was going to get in the way of that goal, not even Sachmo's wonderful smile.

During high school I encountered a teacher who had more than a great influence upon my life. In a pleasant way, he still does. Ralph Kennard was the Poky High School bandleader. About the time I became a "professional" drummer he put me into First Band, where all the good musicians were geeks and real smart. Small as I was, I was on the freshman football team and I thought lowly of becoming a musician. Mister Kennard changed all that.

I don't think Mr. Kennard ever held a drumstick or ever tapped a paradiddle on any drum, as he was a trumpet player. But the man knew what he wanted and how to get it. He gave me a drum book and showed me all 26 drum rudiments. Then he made me practice every spare minute I had available. Drumsticks can be beaten on just about anything and the drummer gets pretty much the same response and feeling as if he's playing on a real drum. But anything is quieter than a real drum!

I set up my drums and cymbals in our basement and began to get even with my three sisters—until Dad said I could only practice during certain times. By the next spring, I had the rudiments down but not quite mastered. The next three years, I took a first in the state music festivals with drum solos, and I can still play "Connecticut Halftime" as well as ever.

Band became my favorite class. The kids in band were smart, talented, and motivated, and became some of my lifetime best friends. We marched in parades, performed concerts and did halftime shows at the football games. An added perk was that I got to play for all the drill teams. They even practiced in short shorts! This caused a problem because all my buddies wanted to come to drill team practice with me, just to fool around. Ha! High school—and short shorts—had a lot to do with the developing testosterone in our young bodies, which none of us understood at the time.

Band was just before lunch. I figured it was because Mr. Kennard didn't want lunch spewed into all the instruments. Often, he got long-winded trying to explain a certain passage to the clarinet section or to the flutes. Sometimes we played soft, pastoral pieces like "Pavane," where the percussion section counted out about 300 bars just to crash the cymbals near the end. This, to us, was boring. And we often miscounted and crashed the cymbals in the wrong place or Mr. Kennard stopped the piece to explain something to the woodwind section after we had counted about 290 bars.

It has always been known by all musicians everywhere that drummers are the clowns of the band. This is fact. During one interminable lecture or some slow, dumb song Roy Miller, Steve Gummersall, and I took several drum straps and hooked them to the belt loops of the trombone section in front of us. Then we hooked the straps to the folding chairs they sat upon. Well, the lunch bell rang and, as always, there was a tear for the door to be first in the lunch line. We drummers were finished with lunch before the rest of the band got sorted out. The next year, band was the first class of the day.

Ralph Kennard was also a Chief Warrant Officer (CWO) in Idaho's Army National Guard. He was the commander of the 45th Army Band, which had about 40 of eastern Idaho's finest young musicians as members. A few might have served in Korea, probably none in World War II. His primary dance band drummer had just graduated from college, and CWO Kennard needed a replacement, quick. He talked me into attending Guard Camp for two weeks as an "attaché." "You could learn a lot," he said, "and besides, you can use the Army's new drum set." I was hooked right there. The 45th Army Band had a new William F. Ludwig drum set with Zildjian cymbals. I'd never seen such a nice set of drums. I went to Guard Camp at Gowan Field in Boise!

I was not quite seventeen, and the National Guard was a "wake up" for me. We got up at 4 a.m. to march a parade, raise the flag, and blow reveille to wake up the rest of the troops. Then breakfast, spit-shine the barracks, and rehearse all morning. Lunch was a welcome break, then more practice, or recording, maybe play a concert, probably march a parade around the camp or visit the tanks in the field for a few marching songs and motivation. There was a parade for taps and then we played for dances at the officer's club or the other service clubs. I usually got to bed about 2 a.m., after the dance job, and suddenly it was four o'clock all over again! I learned to sleep standing up in front of my drum during rehearsals.

After the first week Mister, er uh, Warrant Officer Kennard called me into his office and asked me if I'd like to get paid for all this work. He needed a permanent drummer. I said, "Sure," and signed on the dotted line. I was a couple of months short of seventeen and it was probably illegal to sign on with the Guard at that age. I earned exactly thirteen cents per hour for that Guard Camp. I spent six and a half years in the Idaho National Guard and Army Reserves, which maxed me out on the fogey pay scales for my entire military career. Ever since I joined the Air Force I've earned a hundred or so extra per month, even in retirement!

It seemed that I was always working or playing for dances and didn't have the time to get into trouble with my buddies. Once, even that didn't work. One of my best friends, Jan Sainsbury, was a magician who kept all of us entertained. He performed magic shows around eastern Idaho and he could pick any lock he wanted to pick, but he never committed any crimes.

Well, I guess that depends. One night when I was playing a dance job, Jan picked the lock of the Idaho State University gym so he and all my "good buddies" could go in and skinny-dip in the college pool. They never stole anything or caused any harm, but they got caught!

The Athletic Director, John Vesser, was a friend of my parents. He laid in wait for them, caught them all buck naked, lined them up, and asked each of them their names. They went right down the line answering, "Jan Sainsbury, Denis Yost, Don Gates, Gus Gertsch," and when he got to Tommy Eversole, Tommy gave him my name! "I know your parents!" roared Mr. Vesser, "we'll see what they have to say about this!"

At exactly that time I was sitting behind my drums, behind my dad on the stand at the Green Triangle, the area's largest night club. My performance was witnessed by about 1,000 people dancing to our music. After Dad heard from John Vesser, he cornered me and chewed me out big time! I defended myself, replying that I was playing a dance job at the time, with him, no less. "It doesn't matter," he yelled, "I don't want you doing that ever again!"

"What?"

Chapter Five

The world seemed to be at peace on February 7, 1965. It was a leisurely Sunday. I had been promoted to First Lieutenant just two days earlier but did not get to celebrate, as I was stuck on the alert pad. Some of the guys met their wives at the club for its excellent brunch, a few braved the chilly, damp air of Sacramento in winter to be with their wives and kids in the park next to the alert pad. I slept in, as I had been up quite late listening to the McGrath/Kinney Comedy Hour in the library. The mess hall was closed, except for coffee. I was sharpening up my pocket billiards game when somebody ran past the pool room and hollered, "Hey, you better check the news!"

I ran to the TV room where the reporter said the Viet Cong had attacked a U.S. Army post at some place called Pleiku in the Central Highlands of South Vietnam. Twenty-seven American advisors had been killed. President Johnson was on the television and said that we were not going to put up with them "Veet Cong," and he planned to send some airplanes and more troops over there to show them just what was what!

That piddly-assed little war in the exotic Far East was no concern of mine. They certainly were not going to send our big B-52's over there when a couple of fighter squadrons could do the job. In retrospect, that idea may have been naive. But it was infinitely less naive than the leadership displayed by our President and Secretary of Defense who thought they could play at war instead of politics. They never did understand that war is the failure of politics. They thought it was the other way around and tried to engineer the war to fit that philosophy.

The winter sunshine was bright and the air crisp with February's chill as we huddled in the aft cockpit of our B-52, transferring the nuclear "GO" codes to the aircrew replacing us on alert. After three days on alert, I was ready to bust loose for a couple of days of guaranteed freedom. After that we got to fly. The novelty of tooling around in that big bomber had not yet worn off, I loved flying it. Er, uh, flying in it as a copilot.

Time off was a rare and precious thing in SAC, and I had two days free to do anything I wanted, to go almost anywhere just as long as Jim Gehrig knew where to find me in an emergency. Reno and its gambling tables beckoned, a two-hour drive over the Sierras. My sister, Ellen, who lived in Carson

City, also had a blind date lined up for me with a friend she guaranteed to be as attractive as any woman in Reno.

Three hours after alert changeover, I was counting cards at a blackjack table, waiting for Ellen to meet me for lunch. Being a really cheap gambler, I was only four dollars down when my name, with rank, was paged over the casino's loudspeaker system. This seemed strange to me because no one except Ellen knew I was there, and she would never call me "Lieutenant." She's called me lots of other things but never that. I gathered my chips and left the table.

"Your base called and said for you to get back a-pass," Ellen said over the long distance line from Carson City. She sounded alarmed.

"You mean ASAP?" I asked.

"Yes, that's it. They said to hurry and the highway patrol was notified so you can speed."

"Maybe we're going to war," I joked, knowing the highway patrol doesn't make exceptions, even for people going to war.

"That's not funny, Don," she said. "The man was real serious and he wouldn't tell me what it was all about except that you should get there as soon as you can and to 'drag your bag,' whatever that means."

"Was his name Jim Gehrig?"

"Yes, that's it! A Major Gehrig called."

"They're just playing more of their silly war games," I said. "But it still pisses me off because I was supposed to have two days free, guaranteed."

"Games or not, he sounded serious so you'd better hurry. Call me when you get a chance and we'll all get together another time. My friend will understand—but don't try to take her to bed on the first date, she's my friend, okay?" Ellen knew me.

"Okay," I lied, "I'll call when I can. Bye."

I sped back across the mountains in record time and didn't even see a cop. At my apartment I jumped into my flight suit and grabbed my mobility bag, which crammed with worn-out stuff not fit even for charity. Nuclear or not, this was all a game, remember?

"Briefing's in about fifteen minutes," Jim Gehrig said when I arrived on the alert pad, "but I'm not certain just what's going on yet."

"Oh, great!" I complained, "they ruined our time off just to play silly buggers again."

"I don't think this one's a game," he said. "They downgraded all the alert birds an hour ago."

"Holy shit!" It was all I could say. Something really serious was afoot. When SAC took its B-52's off nuclear alert, it was only for a major happening, and I wondered if it had anything to do with the attack on our guys in Vietnam.

The alert pad swarmed with aircrews, some I hardly even knew. Rumors were rampant. We pilots were usually the last people to hear any scuttlebutt but the Gunner's Rumor Mill was almost as reliable as the Aircrew Wives Intelligence Network. It was amazing what they knew that we did not.

I spotted my gunner, Bill Neville, standing around with a bunch of other gunners and I casually walked over.

"Hey, Gunner," I said, "what's going on?"

"I don't have a clue," he answered. He looked at me as quizzically as I was staring at him. "But I'll bet my life we're heading west."

"You think it's Vietnam?"

"Your guess is as good as mine."

"Damn! All I've got are throwaways in my mobility bag."

"Copilot, will you never learn?" He said this in his best enlisted man's condescending and aloof manner when they were dealing with young copilots. Alone, he would have been himself, nice, but he was with a pack of gunners. They never took their copilots seriously until they had made captain. I'd pinned on my silver first lieutenant bars only a few days earlier, and it would be years before I'd make captain.

We milled around the pad searching for more rumors, and finally seated ourselves in the briefing room designed for about ten aircrews. Every bomber crew on base was there. A couple of staff colonels shuffled around on the briefing platform, but if they knew anything, they weren't talking about it yet.

A large SAC shield sat on an easel on the briefing platform. It showed a mailed fist clutching both an olive branch and some arrows, set on a background of blue with a couple of white clouds for a peaceful effect. This shield was painted on the side of every airplane in SAC. Someone had hidden the shield we usually set on the easel. It showed the mailed fist clutching a castrated, bleeding scrotum. That's how we felt about alert.

Suddenly, someone yelled, "ten-HUT!" We all jumped up and stood at attention until we heard the soft, "At ease." Colonel Van Parker, God to me, marched onto the platform. He wore a most serious face, and I knew right then we were going to Vietnam.

My guess was only about 2,500 miles off. Colonel Parker briefed us on everything he knew. Usually this was reserved for staff colonels, but this briefing would change all of our lives permanently. Colonel Parker, the old combat head, knew this.

"We're going to Guam, but that's classified," said Colonel Parker. "You can tell your families only that we're going to a destination somewhere in the Western Pacific."

"Well that was nice," I thought. The Western Pacific covered about half the earth.

Colonel Jones, our squadron commander, briefed the route: we would aerial refuel off the coast of California and fly a great circle route directly to Guam, no turns. Our tankers would land in Hawaii, refuel, and then fly on to Kadena Air Force Base, Okinawa.

After landing at Andersen Air Force Base, Guam, we could eat dinner and relax for a few hours while the maintenance people refueled our B-52's and loaded them with bombs. Then we would actually fly the first real combat mission in the history of the Strategic Air Command.

The target and the tactics got everyone's attention! We would take off from Guam, meet the tankers once again, this time over the South China Sea for aerial refueling, then fly to Tiger Island off the DMZ, the Demilitarized Zone, of Vietnam. At Tiger Island we would descend to 500 feet, fly up the coast of North Vietnam, turn northwest, over-fly Hanoi at 500 feet with 30 B-52's, pop up to 1500 feet, and destroy the MiG Airfield at Phuc Yen, about ten miles northwest of Hanoi. Whew! Then we'd descend back down to 500 feet in a wide left turn to exit North Vietnam south of Thanh Hoa, climb to 45,000 feet, and fly directly back to Guam.

Even after all these years, Colonel Parker and I are in total agreement, along with most of the people involved in this mission, that had we flown Arc Light One the way it was planned, the Vietnam War would not have begun. Thirty B-52's flying across Hanoi at 500 feet, releasing over 1500 bombs two minutes later, and taking out North Vietnam's primary MiG airfield would have been a whole lot more than impressive. It would have been a "big stick" show of force, the only kind Ho Chi Minh understood.

As it was, millions of people on both sides were killed. During the operation called Linebacker II, in December 1972, which became known as the "Twelve Days of Christmas," the B-52's flew into the Hanoi area for the first time. It took 130 B-52's twelve days to do what our one mission would most definitely have accomplished eight years earlier! Freedom can only be forged with force. It has been proven time and again that freedom cannot be won without the will to fight for it desperately. With weak political leadership, it cannot be accomplished at all.

After the combat deployment briefing, we were told to stay at home and to keep our aircraft commanders informed even if we went to the corner grocery. So, I got my two days off but it didn't make up for the lost date with the girl in Reno.

Military decisions always filter down to the troops in the field late in the afternoon. First, a decision must be made in the White House, and with this president it was usually over luncheon with his Secretary of Defense. The Pentagon is notified and all the generals must be briefed—every one of them has questions. Then the staff colonels must write the messages and open the contingency plans and the majors must codify them and the captains must check everything and the sergeants must type everything and everyone has to initial off on the stuff before it is sent out to the troops in the field.

The Pyramid Alert calls began late in the afternoon of February 10th. This time my mobility bag was packed with all the things I could use in Guam: swimming suit, suntan lotion, an extra pair of sunglasses, new socks and shorts, and all my flight suits. I threw my bag into the car, ready for my great adventure. After interminable briefings on the alert pad, we were ready to go to war.

At dawn on the eleventh of February, 1965, the first airplane rolled down Mather's runway to begin the deployment. A cell of three KC-135 tankers took off at one-minute intervals, followed by a cell of three B-52's. Our crew was number two in the second cell of bombers, and we climbed to an initial cruising altitude of 35,000 feet behind our cell of tankers.

Long before we leveled off, our jet engines began to draw white contrails across the clear blue winter sky. We coasted out just north of San Francisco and were followed by our sister B-52F wing from Barksdale Air Force Base, Louisiana. Destination? Somewhere in the Western Pacific. Sixty-four large jet airplanes and 384 jet engines painted the sky white with contrails.

Passing the Faralon Islands, our last view of American soil, the tankers spread out into a three-mile-wide echelon formation. We nuzzled up behind our tanker, and the boomer stuck his colorful probe into our receptacle and fed us fuel until our tanks were brim full. I logged every pound in my fuel log. What a chore! Don't ever let a B-52 copilot tell you he flies the airplane! We lie notoriously about that, especially around women. One flight pattern around the flagpole once a month is enough for us. Log the fuel, Copilot! And shut up. I never once got to touch the yoke during an aerial refueling.

When the refueling was completed, the tankers climbed and turned away from us, heading toward Hawaii. The monotony of flying across the Pacific Ocean was quickly realized, there was nothing but water ahead of us for the next 13 hours. As the fuel burned off and our weight decreased, we stepped our altitude up gradually until we reached 45,000 feet.

Far below, cloud decks rolled across the ocean in patterned waves, their dazzling whiteness too intense to stare at for long. The sky above was a deep cerulean blue as we raced the sun across the Pacific. I was both excited and bored, as every minute carried me further west than I'd ever been—Chrome Dome's don't count because we didn't land, we went home! I scanned the instruments, took fuel readings, gave oxygen checks to the gunner, and watched the endless sky merge with the sea of clouds below.

In pilot training they said flying was simply hours of boredom with moments of sheer terror. I had never experienced a single moment of sheer terror, only boredom. In a B-52 at 45,000 feet, a copilot could go out of his skull with boredom. This was just like a Chrome Dome mission.

Each throttle had two little white knobs connected to the same throttle shaft. One set of eight knobs was close together, allowing the pilot to grab a whole handful of knobs to "hand fly" the B-52, usually for takeoff and landing. Above and slightly forward of the hand-flying-type knobs was another set used when cruising on autopilot, which was almost all the time. Two knobs, for engines four and five, were raised even higher so the pilots could make minor airspeed adjustments without having to constantly reset all eight engines. Once the engines were set on a particular power percentage and the throttle friction was on, a small movement on the two center throttles kept the airspeed correct. Once that was finished, there was no more flying by either pilot, just sitting and watching. Boooredom! I'd love to do it once again, just one more time.

On the instrument panel in front of the throttles were 40 round, glass-enclosed dials, five different readings for each engine. Forty instruments to watch constantly just to tell you how your engines were running. Nobody wanted to spend their lives staring at those things—the trick was to glance at the panel, and if one needle was not aligned with its partners, then you take a closer look. On takeoff the co-pilot's eyes were busy scanning these instruments but during cruise his mind played diabolical games with his eyes.

With nothing much to look at, the eyes flitted from one instrument to another, feeding repetitive information to the brain and boring it even further. This caused the brain to tell the eyes to "go get a life" and find something to keep it from being so bored. It was a vicious cycle that drove most copilots around the bend but it never seemed to bother the AC's. Jim Gehrig was never bored, he didn't have to take fuel readings!

As the fuel burned out of the tanks the airplane got lighter, which caused a slight shift in the CG, and when this happened we had to adjust the two top throttles again, which resulted in one or the other of us continually playing with those two throttles.

Anyway, that is how a copilot flies a B-52. He logs fuel readings, stares at the multitude of instruments until his eyeballs fry, and watches the unchanging sky go by.

On the center of the yoke was a large plastic cap, in-
laid in grays and blues that proudly stated, "B-52 STRA-
TOFORTRESS." I fooled around with it until it fell off into
my hand. Inside was written, "SAC SUCKS." Some other
copilot had been cruising around at high altitude for too
long. This struck me as funny and I couldn't help laughing,
so I showed it to Jim but he didn't think it was funny, and
I thought maybe he was the one who had been cruising
around up here for too long.

It was time once again for the gunner's oxygen check.
"Gunner, Copilot, oxygen check." I waited. He was asleep
again. "Uh . . . Gunner, Copilot, oxygen check," a little louder. Nothing. Now, I wasn't getting worried, but the gunner's
well-being was my responsibility, and if he died from lack of
oxygen I'd never forgive myself. I tapped the rudders gently
to wake him, knowing that the g-force translates through
the plane to seven times what we felt up front. He might
bounce around a bit but it was sure to wake him. I waited . . .

"Goddamn it, Copilot!" he roared. "I was taking a piss
and spilled the bag all over my leg!"

Embarrassed, I glanced over at Jim, who was laughing
out loud.

"Excuse me," I shouted to Jim, not using the interphone,
"I'm going downstairs to take a leak. You want anything?"

"Take one for me too, Copilot," he said with a grin. I
knew that when I got back he'd ask me if I took a leak for
him too, and he'd laugh again. I couldn't wait to upgrade
from copilot.

As I passed the Electronic Warfare station I saw that Jim Erbes was asleep, as usual, with his oxygen mask dangling and his mouth agape. I wished I had some gum, and made a mental note to get some more. Bill Hart was asleep with his chin on his palm and his elbow on the navigation table. Terry was buried in Bill's radar set. I knew these guys. Knew what they would do in almost any situation. It wasn't so much that they were all so predictable, rather that we grew so close that it sometimes got scary. That was why I loved to slip gum into Jim Erbes' sleeping mouth. It was, so far, the only secret I had for my very own with these guys.

We droned on across the Pacific. The B-52 in front of us gushed contrails that slid under our nose like white railroad tracks. To watch them for long was hypnotizing. We flew one mile behind and 500 feet above the B-52 in front of us, and there was another in the same place behind and above us. This was a B-52 cell formation, one mile behind, 500 feet above. Cells followed each other at four-minute intervals. This formation was used throughout the Vietnam War.

Flying a mile behind the plane in front of us felt almost like close formation. His wings seemed to stretch clear across our wind-screen, and I recalled that the Wright Brothers' first flight was far shorter than the wingspan of a B-52. From above and behind, the six-story tail blended into his fuselage and caused the B-52 to look more like a flying wing. I know, these weird thoughts were the product of boredom even though the scenery was magnificent.

What scenery? Clouds and water below, sky above, and the fuel control panel in front of me.

"Midway Island is just off our left," Terry said over the interphone. "We're coming up to take a look." In seconds, two navigators and the EWO were in line to take a peek over the pilot's dashboard at Midway. But it was covered in clouds.

"Copilot, why didn't you tell us there was cloud cover?" complained Bill Hart. It was a way of life for us copilots.

"You didn't ask," I said. I raised my seat and pretended to look for the island, imagining the great sea battle that changed the course of World War II. Just think what we could have done against those Japanese carriers with even one B-52. I wondered what role we might play in the little war coming up in Vietnam.

A couple of hours later Terry said, "We're abeam Wake Island."

"The cloud cover's gone," I answered before even looking outside with my sun-fried eyes, "but I can't see the island. Where is it?"

"About ten o'clock low. Can you see it?"

The sun had passed us, and it reflected off the millions of waves shimmering 45,000 feet below in the dazzling display of the western Pacific. The sea was blinding.

"Don't bother to come up," said Jim Gehrig, finally breaking hours of silence. "We can't see anything in the wave reflections anyway."

At that altitude, the sky above was a dark blue, and

when I stared hard at the horizon I thought I could see a slight curve in the earth's distant surface. But it was the dashboard clock my eyes kept straying toward, my brain counting each minute until my sore ass could once more walk the earth. I'd had very little sleep, although there was plenty of time for it. My mind simply would not shut down and let me rest whenever it was flying. Something inside didn't want me to miss a thing in life.

Jim Gehrig finally tapped me on the arm and pointed down at eleven o'clock. There, surrounded by the shimmering, golden-wave reflections from the lowered sun, was the dark, hourglass shape of the entire island of Guam. From our altitude the sight was incredible.

B-52's on nuclear alert. Hound Dog missiles are under the wings.

Courtesy of Colonel Van R. Parker

B-52's on an Elephant Walk after a Coco Alert.

Courtesy of Colonel Van R. Parker

Don Harten as a 2nd Lieutenant a few months before the ARC LIGHT ONE mission.

A very rare formation flown by Mather B-52's. Normal formation throughout the Vietnam War was a cell of three, one mile in trail and 500 feet above the guy in front.

Courtesy of Colonel Ralph W. Jones

The B-17 Moonlight Cocktail was shot down over Austria during World War II. The survivors spent the rest of the war in Stalag POW camps around Germany. Chuck Andermann is a 2nd Lieutenant, in back row at far right.

Courtesy of Theresa Andermann

Chuck Andermann at his work station in the Radar Navigator's seat in the basement of a B-52.

Don Harten's sisters and cousins at the farm.

Gunslinger and his steed. The first time Don rode this thing he coasted down a hill and "ran over" the first car he encountered. First rides have always been a problem with this guy.

Don and sister, Ellen, who retains that wonderful smile. A cavalier attitude is displayed by the young pilot to be. The neat uniform confirmed his desire to fly—and to make girls smile.

Shortly after author's first ejection . . . from a moving car. As usual, he landed on his head.

Don is the little kid on a leash shortly after ejecting himself from a moving car!

We wowed them with "Big Noise from Winetka": Don's performance at the Green Triangle, the area's largest night club, was witnessed by about 1,000 people dancing to the music.

Andersen AFB, Guam, in early 1965. Within a year the base was paved with B-52's. At the end of the runway the cliff dropped 600 feet to the Pacific Ocean.

A Mather B-52F dropping on a Viet Cong stronghold.

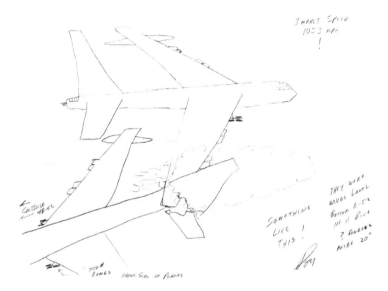

Author (inept) sketch of how two B-52's came together.

A Mather B-52 returns from the ARC LIGHT ONE mission. Without bombs and fuel, the wings ride high and the outrigger landing gear is off the ground.

General Jimmy Stewart flew a combat mission with us on our second tour. Colonel Parker is at far right.

Dave Roeder gives a baseball cap with the "Iron Dukes" patch on it to Brigadier General Jimmy Stewart. Dave designed the patch just so he could meet General Stewart. (That's a lie!)

Survivors of the ARC LIGHT ONE head-on midair collision (L-R): Chuck Andermann, Pete Nichols, Jim Erbes, Don Harten, Jay Collier. Pete became our Aircraft Commander after Jim Gehrig was killed in midair. The luxury digs in this photo, taken during second combat tour, are in the SAC Compound barracks at Andersen AFB, Guam.

Lt. Col. Ralph Jones holds the Memorial Wreath, which was dropped from a Mather B-52 over the spot of the midair collision during the memorial services half a world away in the Mather AFB Chapel.

Courtesy of Colonel Ralph W. Jones

Crew E-45 in front of *Parker's Pride* after landing from a second combat tour. We had just returned from Guam to Mather. This was the last flight of a silver "F" model out of Guam. Pictured are Pete Nichols, Don Harten, Chuck Andermann, Bernie Dowes, Jim Erbes, and Charlie McCarthy.

B-52F #034 *Parker's Pride* Mather AFB, CA2. Hound Dog missile is under wing.

Lt. Col. Jones gives Lt. Co. Andermann an award.

Lt. Col. Jones awards an Air Medal to Don. The SAC patch is on the side of the B-52.

Chapter Six

We departed the extreme cold of the stratosphere and descended into the warm humidity of the tropics. The airplane, having been cold-soaked for 14 hours, took its time warming, and the cockpit fogged up almost completely. Moisture condensed and it began to rain inside the cockpit! Actually, it dripped from the ceiling where it pooled at low points in the piping or bulkheads. Everything got wet. I turned the defog system on full blast just so we could see outside.

Guam Approach Control vectored us on a slow, low-level tour up the island to Andersen Air Force Base on the northeast point of land. Jim flew the plane while I called the checklist and watched this beautiful, tropical island with its white coral beaches pass by underneath. Small villages, with whitewashed, two-steepled churches and houses, capped with corrugated steel roofs, were scattered among the countless palm trees waving our arrival. Reef-protected lagoons of the very lightest blue were surrounded by the dark, sea-green of the deep ocean.

We floated down onto the runway and coasted to the end, fifth in a very long line of B-52's arriving every minute. The tower directed us to the far side of the field, where we parked and shut down the engines. Exhausted, we exited the bomber just as the sun reflected its last rays off the tropical, flamingo-colored clouds that drifted in the gentle breeze over the island. The temperature was perfect, exactly what an island paradise was supposed to be. Only feet away, on the other side of a tall chain-link fence, was the jungle. I'd never before seen jungle. It was full of coconut palms and all the exotic plants I'd ever imagined. And the history! Bombers took off for Japan in World War II from this very hardstand only twenty years earlier.

An Air Force-blue, six-pack pickup waited for us. We "dragged our bags" to the pickup and left our flight gear in the plane, as we expected to return to our own B-52 for the combat mission in a few hours. The pickup driver, a young airman, drove us to the base side of the runway.

"Where you people from?" he asked, friendly like.

The navigators were chatting like crows, the AC didn't answer, and the gunner looked away. I did not want our crew to seem too unfriendly so I answered him.

"From the States."

"I've never seen so many B-52's in my life," he said.

"Neither have I," I said truthfully.

"But you guys fly them all the time," he said.

"Yeah, but I've never seen so many in one place at the same time." The AC nudged me in the ribs and it ended the conversation. This sleepy little island was going to be awakened for the first time since we had defeated the Japanese.

The driver dropped us off at a blue, two-story concrete barracks where we got our rooms. Five officers, one crew, in a two-man, freezing cold, air-conditioned room. The gunners were next door, only three to a room, their "Enlisted Man's Protective Association" working well.

I threw my bag onto my chosen bunk, home for the next several months, and headed for the john. Inside, lounging like he owned the place, was a five-inch (I swear) cockroach! He scurried behind the toilet. I never saw him again but I always wondered if he could have stolen our mobility bags. The room was actually quite clean since we had daily maid service.

The AC returned from a short meeting and said we were cleared to go to the officer's club, a couple of blocks away, for dinner. None of us bothered to take a shower. We must have smelled like a herd of goats after our 15-hour flight.

The club was brand new and beautifully decorated. We ate an excellent dinner, without wine since we were expected to fly again in a few hours. Of course, crew rest had been waived for combat. We were not allowed to drink alcohol 12 hours prior to flying or smoke within 15 feet of the aircraft, but we joked about not drinking within 50 feet of the airplane or smoking within 12 hours of flight. Shortly, we would pack our butts back into our bombers and fly another 12 hours to drop bombs on North Vietnam.

Unexpectedly, a colonel, whom none of us knew but who seemed to have a handle on things, called for everyone's attention. He said the mission had been delayed, we could all have a beer. The club erupted into a loud cheer and everyone scrambled for the bar. About 30 aircrews, times five men per crew, clamored for drinks, thirsty after the long deployment. But it took forever to belly up to the bar. I lasted for only one beer, then had to search out my new home in the dark, a small room somewhere in a huge complex of blue barracks on a base I'd never seen before.

The white coral sand at Tarague Beach (pronounced Ta rah' ghee) is a fine powder, cool to walk upon in the brilliant tropical sunlight. At water's edge the gentle waves lap at your feet and inside the barrier reef, the lagoon is so clear you can see underwater for a hundred feet or more. Thousands of tropical fish make their homes here, safe from the treacherous open sea beyond. The reef, a few hundred yards from shore, is where the big waves crash and spend themselves, breaking into ripples inside the lagoon. The continuous roar carries to the beach in a peaceful rhythm that is soothing to the soul. Without doubt, Tarague is one of the finest, most beautiful beaches in the world. (Secret's out!)

Our combat mission had been delayed indefinitely so, without immediate duties, we were free to go anywhere as long as we "logged out." The first thing on my agenda was to acquire a diving mask, snorkel, and swim fins before the Base Exchange was sold out. The second and only other thing on that agenda was to hit the beach!

An old, Air Force-blue school bus departed the Base Exchange every half-hour for the trip down the 600-foot cliff road through the gently stirring palms to that fabulous beach. I was so enthralled by the view that I never worried that the school bus could lose its brakes. I'd just die happily in paradise.

Rota, about 20 miles away, just north of Guam in the Marianas chain, could be seen from the top of the cliff. North of Rota lay Tinian, where the B-29's took off to drop their atomic bombs on Japan to end World War II.

For as far as one could see in all directions was the blue of the ocean, topped with fluffy cotton balls of cloud that floated gently on the tropical breeze. The green of the palms was as green as anything ever got, all trimmed by the stark white beach and the white-blue lagoon.

Hidden in the palms behind the beach at Tarague was a tiny hot dog stand run by a small Guamanian man of indeterminate age. He served ice-cold San Miguel beer, soda pop, and sandwiches, and he could husk a coconut faster than you could get your money out to pay him.

The sweet coconut milk was often more refreshing than beer or soda. Coconuts lay on the ground everywhere, under so many palm trees you could not count them. It was comfortably cool in the mottled shadows of the palms.

I spent hours floating face down, watching the under-water creatures watching me. The large aquarium fish were friendly but wary. They wouldn't let you touch them but if you had something for them to eat they would carefully swim close, acting like they were only interested and then, zip, they would grab it right out of your hand and swim off to a safe distance to eat it. Two layers of skin peeled off my back before I began to turn brown in the tropical sun.

The beach was about a mile long with rock outcrop-pings at both ends. I love to explore so I climbed over rocks, swimming sometimes to get around a point of land. I bought a diver's knife and poked around the rocks to find things I never expected to see anywhere on this earth. A lit-tle fish with a head that was bigger than the rest of his body had fins he used for running from one tidal pool, across the rocks and coral, to another pool. Sometimes he would stand on his fins and watch me with his head crooked to see what I was going to do. The sea was filled with creatures even more curious about me than I about them.

A sea cucumber spit his white tentacles at me. Tiny barnacles clung to the rocks where even typhoon waves could not knock them loose. I fell in love with Guam, only to return many years later to find Paradise Lost. The Japa-nese had bought up the island, erecting high-rise hotels everywhere and charging a prohibitive price per night for only a small room. They may have lost the big war, but I'm not certain we won it.

Normally, an Air Force base can handle one bomber

wing and its attendant tankers, and maintenance and administrative support. Andersen had its compliment of permanent party people who, by the way, enjoyed life and seemed to party permanently. A detachment of ten B-52's from Biggs Air Force Base in El Paso, Texas, was the only other temporary duty outfit there at the time. They were always on rotational nuclear alert, so we didn't see much of them.

Our own aircrew "families" grew even closer and, to some, it seemed that every copilot had his hip welded to his AC's hip, we were that close. But in Guam we also began to feel our freedom and got to know our "cousins," other copilots. Copilots had a lot in common in that we all hated the fuel curve! I began to pal around with guys like Dave Roeder and Jim Marshall. Dave and I have been close friends for all these years and I'd like to have known Jim much better. Jim was a dead ringer for Tyrone Power, the movie star, and he was a really nice guy.

The senior noncommissioned officers on base were the first to realize the serious problem of two newly arrived squadrons of horny bomber crews. They ordered their young daughters to stay close to home and away from the beach until we redeployed back to the States. But it would be eight long years before the B-52's would eventually leave Guam.

In those first couple of weeks I learned to walk. Walking was the only way to get around unless you waited for the shuttle bus and that almost always took longer than walking. In the morning we'd walk about a mile to the Base Operations Snack Bar, the most popular place on base, for breakfast and a copy of the *Stars and Stripes* newspaper. Overlooking the flight line, we ate and read the news of the developing Vietnam War and we watched airplanes take off on their way to Vietnam. Until 1968 the vast majority of Americans supported our action in the war but it had not, as yet, really started. The day after we arrived, headlines shouted that the Viet Cong had attacked some place called Qui Nhon and killed 23 Americans! Vietnam was still too far away for me to comprehend yet, but it was getting closer each day.

The Base Exchange sold everything from pearl rings to stateside clothes. I bought a beautiful full service of Noritake china, I don't know why, but the box fit nicely under my bunk. (My ex-wife still uses it.)

Sometimes we spent hot afternoons in the air-conditioned bar of the officer's club drinking cold San Miguel, an outstanding Philippine beer. We played "ship, captain, and crew," a fun dice game for the drinks. The club served excellent dinners and, for a change of pace, we often scrounged a rusted out "Guam Bomb" and drove off base, where we found the true flavor of the island. The price was right and the food was outstanding. We ate delicious seafood barbecue and water buffalo steaks until we could hold no more. It was the first time I'd weighed over 125 pounds in my life!

A nine-hole golf course lay only a ten-minute walk from our quarters. The shuttle bus always took half an hour to arrive. I have never figured out people who waited for the bus to go play golf. The course had an excellent driving range and a small putting green. We rented clubs and carried iced beer and soda around in the pouches. Fairways wandered seaward through the palm groves and a few of the greens overlooked breathtaking views of the sea below. Sometimes we teed up old balls and drove them down into the ocean as far as Jack Nicklaus ever could on level ground.

Except for its airfield complex, Andersen Air Force Base was a giant lawn. One type of grass had wide, serrated blades and when it was touched or walked upon it curled up into a withered-looking weed. After a minute or so, it slowly opened its blades and got friendly again, like some of the timid, curious fish at the beach. When touched again the grass blades took even longer to open up, like they had little brains and knew we were playing a game with them.

The remains of old World War II Quonset hut buildings were scattered around the base, most with just a foundation and a few pipes sticking out where the walls used to be. The old officer's club had been torn down, and when the wind whispered through the palms I could imagine the ghosts of that era singing war songs. When I returned to Guam in 1988, more time had passed since the Vietnam War than from World War II until 1965! I, too, had become a ghost.

We often took the bus into Agana where numerous corrugated iron-roofed taverns stood close to the water's edge. Shrimp cocktails and San Miguel beer became the staple lunch, along with a game of shuffleboard, which was Guam's national sport. Our aircrew's favorite bar was the South Seas Club, where Rachael San Nichols, the gunner's new girlfriend, tended bar. On the wall behind the bar hung a framed navigator's chart used by ancient South Sea Islanders to sail between islands in open canoes. Stuck here and there on the chart were small stones and short lengths of bamboo that apparently indicated stars or constellations. None of our navigators could figure it out. I never thought of trying.

Most of Guam is a 600-foot-high plateau. The sea has eaten into the cliffs in many places and lagoons formed. One of the cliffs, north of the capital Agana, was called "Lover's Leap." There are lots of lover's leaps all over the world but this one was significant in that people really leapt off it. Near the end of World War II, hundreds of Japanese and their sweethearts jumped onto the rocks below rather than face the terror promised them by their commanders when the Americans arrived to take back the island.

It was said there were still Japanese soldiers hiding out on the south part of Guam, and in the 1980s one of them turned himself in after his buddy had died. I sometimes wonder what they thought about the B-52's that thundered over their hideouts in the jungle—huge planes without propellers on their eight engines. The terrors that were hidden in their souls about what we American's would do to them if they ever came out of hiding must have haunted them every night. With all those bombers flying around

Guam they surely thought we were still at war with Japan. When Pearl Harbor was attacked they had been young men, and when they finally surrendered they would return to be cheered in Japan as heroes for carrying on the war for some 40 years after it was over.

South of Agana, the U.S. Naval Station tended nuclear submarines, and east of Agana, up the hill overlooking the sea, was the Agana Naval Air Station. It doubled as a civilian airport for a few airliners going to and from the Orient. Their officers' club was often populated with stewardesses (now flight attendants) laying over during their long flights of hauling troops to Vietnam. They never stayed more than one night, if that, so we left them for the Navy to hustle.

After a week or two of waiting for combat orders, Colonel Kline decided we needed to keep up our flying proficiency. Every day a B-52 would take off and fly around the Marianas and return after a couple of hours to shoot touch-and-go landings. Then it taxied to Base Operations and downloaded all the navigators, along with the gunner, and uploaded about eight AC's and copilots. Then we would take off and fly around the flagpole, and after one guy got his takeoff and landing, he got out of the seat and another guy got in to do the same thing. When everyone had had a takeoff and a landing, we taxied back to Base Ops and got out, and another load of pilots got in and did the same thing. We quickly filled our annual training squares doing this.

It worked well for about a week until everybody had

their landings for the year. After that, Colonel Kline had to think of something else for us to do besides loafing at the beach. It drove him nuts to watch us enjoy ourselves when normally we were used to working about 12 days per week.

One day the nuclear missile submarine USS *Tecumseh* came into Agana to change crews and do a bit of maintenance. Their Gold Crew had finished three months under water, waiting for a nuclear war to begin; now they were docked to changeover with Blue Crew. Our four-day nuclear alert tours seemed like doing hard time in jail until I talked with some of those guys.

Somebody wrangled an exchange with them, a tour of a B-52 for a tour of a nuclear sub! I think we got the best part of that deal because you can tour a B-52 in no time. Nobody is interested in any of the cockpit instruments, especially not the fuel control panel! But they all asked, "How big is that bomb bay?" For us, a visit inside a nuclear sub was the trip of a lifetime.

The captain showed us "Sherwood Forest" where steel missile silos encased war-ready Polaris missiles tipped with nuke warheads. The reactor room was eerie, just like in the movies. In the control room they "flew" the sub just like an airplane but the captain didn't get to handle the control yoke, some low-ranking seaman got to do the flying. The captain, however, was no copilot. Somebody else got coffee for him.

On board, we had lunch in the officer's mess, an incredibly tiny galley that also served as a card room, library, and whatever else there was to do during free time on a submarine cruise. It would be like living in a B-52 cockpit for three months on alert! Man, their entire officer's open mess was about the same size as the library on our alert pad back home! I couldn't live that way, and don't know how they did. Had I gone Navy and washed out of pilot training they would have made me the fuel systems officer on a sub! I'd have been a raving maniac within a week! Give me the good old sky any day—and Tarague Beach.

Paradise lacked only one thing: women. And then we discovered the Navy nurses! Navy Agana, the air station, had a hospital with a whole dorm full of nurses. Single ones. I'm not certain who discovered whom but it wasn't long before some of us got together. Beach parties in the evening were like a college fraternity party where we barbecued and swam in the moonlight. One nurse showed me a secluded bay where a tethered raft floated about a hundred yards from the beach. The swim was easy. On the raft was a glass window for watching the creatures below, and we laid there staring for hours at sea urchins crawling along the bottom of the lagoon on long, black pins.

To keep us busy, and especially to keep our heads into reality since the trance of tropical life was constantly calling us, Colonel Kline decided to give us a briefing every morning at 0900 hours—nine o'clock to those of us who were beginning to lose touch. With nothing much going on, the briefing usually lasted about half an hour and then we were free until the next morning. This at least kept us with one foot on the ground. However, there was one guy I won't name who lost it all. But he sure had fun going out.

He got carried away with the island life, with a married woman, and with cheap booze. Unfortunately he missed a briefing or something and was restricted to the base. During this restriction he got drunk and wrecked his girl-friend's car while driving drunk, and they sent him home immediately. Years later I bumped into him in Bangkok, drunk again, an old man reduced in grade to enlisted status to finish out his 20 years. It was truly sad because he was a witty and brilliant fellow who let the booze get the best of him. I wondered how much of the blame could be laid on the enchantment of that tropical paradise.

Bill Neville spent all of his free time at the South Seas Club, playing shuffleboard and hustling Rachael San Nich-ols, who could have run for Miss Guam. One glance and I wanted to meet her sister. These old-head gunners knew right where to find the action and, unlike officers, they never hesitated. The officers in our group were mostly fam-ily men who searched out the finer restaurants rather than the women, and most of them wouldn't even fool around at a convention of prostitutes!

One day we were driving back from the Navy base when it started to sprinkle. Terry was driving and he slowed to 15 miles per hour on the coral dust surface of the road, which was slicker than black ice when it got wet. A big, black Guam Bomb passed us going about 25 miles per hour and, when he turned in after passing, he skidded out of control, spun across the highway, and rammed into the guardrail. Nobody was hurt and the Bomb wasn't even dented. A couple of young sailors hopped out laughing. But from the opposite direction, an older Guamanian couple, in a white car, driving no faster than 20 miles per hour, could not stop in time and skidded into the side of the Bomb. It barely dented the Bomb's door. We stopped to see if anyone possibly could have been hurt.

The olive-skinned, wrinkled little Guamanian man was holding his hand over the heart of his wife in the passenger seat. She appeared unconscious, and I tried to help her. They could not have impacted the Bomb at more than 15 miles per hour but the woman had been thrown forward and had hit her head on the windshield. Apparently a broken splinter of glass entered her brain. She died in my arms. I was devastated. If ever there was a case for seat belts, this was it! Nobody was really at fault but I'll never forget the scene.

Almost every night we attended a movie at one of the four open-air theaters on base. It was like going to a drive-in movie without your car. The local people, even the kids, all brought umbrellas. Logically, none of us thought to include umbrellas in our mobility bags. It rained every night in the middle of the flick, and we got soaked, but we continued sitting in the warm, gentle breezes, shivering until the movie was over. Then we'd rush back to the barracks, and the icy air conditioner would freeze us even further. It seemed the only time I was really warm in Guam was at the beach or playing golf.

The Air Force owned a large, sport fishing boat and docked it at the Navy base. It was meant for our morale. In Paradise? It paid for itself handsomely with only a ten-dollar charge per person for a day of deep sea fishing, bring your own lunch, thank you. Some of us went out for a day and we cruised around the island, waiting for a big game fish to strike our bait. I laid on the bow and stared down into the bow wave, daydreaming. It was magically hypnotic. Dolphins joined us to play in the bow wave of the boat. These beautiful mammals had fun showing off, and they knew I loved it. They bounced around, jumping in the waves, taking turns letting the bow wave push them.

Flying fish jumped out of the water and coasted for a hundred feet or more in the "ground effect" just above the waves. When their airspeed slowed, they would fold their little fin-wings and dive straight into the face of a wave.

The Soviets kept a fishing "trawler," a spy ship, posted three miles off the port of Agana. When the B-52's arrived he changed position to a point about three miles off the end of the Andersen runway. We waved to each other whenever we passed, knowing we were mortal enemies and yet, here we were being friendly toward each other. However, some of us waved the internationally understood one-finger salute! The trawler stayed three miles off Andersen's runway throughout the Vietnam War.

We took turns sitting in the deck-bolted fishing seats,

waiting for something to strike. I caught a barracuda, who was a real fighter, but the line was weighed for sharks or marlin and he didn't have a chance. The boat's captain stunned him and threw him onto ice in the aft hold.

Together, we caught three, yard-long fish and when we got to port the captain tossed them onto the grass beside the dock. I asked what he planned to do with them and was appalled to hear he was going to throw them back into the water for the crabs to eat. I couldn't stand the thought that such beautiful fish lived just to be caught and discarded.

I carried them to the Andersen Officers' Club, wrapped in white paper, and gave them to the chef, who seemed amazed at my action but pleased to give the men a treat like this. He cooked them in a delicious sauce and served them on a bed of ice to everyone in the bar. I thought my barracuda tasted the best but, of course, that was only my opinion.

Some of the guys talked me into going scuba diving outside the reef but I had to fly that day and was forced to decline. I was thankful because I have a secret fear of sharks. I'd rather fly anyway. The guys came back with tales that would have dampened my enthusiasm for even the lagoon at Tarague Beach. About 50 feet down, just outside the reef, a shark approached and circled them. He closed the circle with every lap until they could almost reach out and touch his nose. Had I been there, I certainly would have gone bonkers and shot to the surface. The shark, probably thinking I was a tasty seal about 6,000 miles off course, would have eaten me before I broke the waves. Finally though, he left, apparently thinking that other, smaller fish would be easier and more delectable than my friends. Sharks terrify me!

Four months after we arrived in Guam, Bill Hart retired, Terry Lowry upgraded to Radar Navigator, and we got ourselves a brand-new navigator, Jay Collier, who was fresh out of navigation school. The first thing Jay and I settled was who had the earliest date of rank—he outranked me by two days. I still had the shit details for the crew! I don't know why we never recruited gunners to be gofers, probably because of the "Gunner's Benevolent and Protective Association," which was the first politically correct organization in history. Besides, we could never find any of them anyway. They only showed up for scheduled meetings or flights. I knew I could always find Bill Neville down at the South Seas Club almost anytime. Anyway, I continued my job as the crew errand boy.

A new navigator does not have the same problems adjusting to crew life as does a copilot. When we are flying, almost everything a copilot says and does is heard over the interphone and his mistakes are visible! A navigator sits in the downstairs station with the radar nav, and they shout at each other over the noises of the black boxes and spinning gyros rather than use the interphone, which is mostly kept clear for the pilot's use. If a navigator is slow to catch on or makes stupid mistakes, it stays between him and the radar nav. He is immune to the visibility that exposes new copilots to exaggerated, unmerciful teasing. Sometimes we copilots felt as dumb as an avalanche of lemmings.

Chapter Seven

The night before Armed Forces Day in June, 1965, we flew a six-hour go around the East Philippine Sea to give our new navigator, Jay Collier, some practice over open ocean. Jay was a personable sort and he got along well with everyone, even me—after I forgave him for outranking me by two days! That night we were scheduled to contact one of our tankers out of Kadena Air Force Base in Okinawa for a night aerial refueling. This mission was memorable in two ways: first, as an omen of things to come and second, because we were the first B-52 aircrew ever to lose all four engines on one side, one of the worst emergency nightmares imaginable in a B-52 and the one we worked on every time when we flew the emergency procedures simulator.

We took off at about ten o'clock that night, tooled

around over the ocean, and finally met our tanker about halfway to Okinawa. Maintenance had replaced the oil filters on all the engines with a new, supposedly more efficient type. Along with my fuel readings, I was to log oil pressure readings for an evaluation. At about midnight one of the oil pressure gauges showed a large drop in pressure. I tapped Jim's shoulder and pointed, and we shut the engine down before it caused any damage. Jim Erbes reported the engine shutdown to Andersen on the HF radio and none of us thought anything more about it. After all, we had seven more engines.

We hooked up with the tanker and about halfway through the refueling I noticed that another oil gauge had dropped to zero. I told Jim and shut the engine down. Engines seven and eight were now in windmill. Jim told the tanker to discontinue the refueling because we now had an emergency. So we disconnected and dropped off the tanker. The tanker turned left, which they always did when we disconnected. But we had been in a right turn! To Jim it looked like the tanker turned away when he only rolled out level! We were still in a thirty-degree bank.

Jim wanted to expedite the turn back to Guam and he put us in a right bank of what he thought was forty-five degrees. I got out my fuel log and when I looked up we were in a steep bank and falling out of the sky! I grabbed the yoke and shouted to Jim just as he saw what was happening. We fell. With lots of left rudder and both of us on the yoke we rolled out after losing only a few thousand feet.

At night, unless you watch the attitude indicator, you cannot tell which way is up. Same thing happens in inclement weather.

On the way back to Guam, Terry told us about the time he was a young navigator on a B-36H, which had six giant pusher props and four jet engines outboard of the props that they used for extra takeoff thrust. For cruise at altitude they routinely shut down the jets and only restarted them for landing. About two hundred miles from Japan they thought it might be funny to notify approach control that they were coming in with four engines shut down. The Japanese went ape and alerted air-sea rescue. Panic ensued until one of the controllers calmly asked if they were an "H" model B-36 with the four jets shutdown. "Roger." That plane had ten engines aboard and could land at light weight with only two pushers going if need be. The B-52, on the other hand, crashes without a minimum of four engines running—and for this it must be at light weight with the fuel tanks nearly empty and no bombs on board.

A couple of hundred miles out of Guam, we lost oil pressure on engine number five and I shut it down. We notified the Command Post that we thought the new filters were clogging up and that we just hoped we could make it back before all the engines quit. From altitude we began a long, slow descent with the remaining engines retarded and we asked for a vector to a short final approach, knowing that if we lost two more engines the bomber would no longer stay in the air and we'd have to exchange it for parachutes.

As we turned onto the short final, Jim extended the landing gear and the oil pressure on number six fell to zero. I told him that I was not going to shut it down until we had the landing assured. You can let a jet engine run for about one minute with zero oil pressure if you don't move the throttle. Otherwise, the number six bearing, inside the engine, will freeze up and cause the engine to self-destruct and possibly explode. In a single-engine jet fighter there is no choice but to try and avoid hospitals and schoolyards, which seem to attract out-of-control jets. At least that's what the newsies say. In an emergency, a pilot cannot tell a hospital or schoolyard from anything else but if the pilot rides it in he becomes a dead hero—unless he hits the school or hospital.

I held the number six throttle steady and dropped the flaps as Jim maneuvered onto final approach. We glided down a high angle final and, as we crossed the runway threshold, I pulled number six to off. Jim let the plane sink onto the runway and we coasted to the end with four engines out on one side!

We turned off the runway and, because the display aircraft for Armed Forces Day were parked on the taxiway, the tower told us to turn around and taxi back up the runway we just came down in order to get to our parking area. We protested and they insisted. We simply could not turn to the left. Jim was so mad he threatened to shut the thing down right there. The people at Andersen did not yet understand what it took to operate a B-52. Ground pounders have never understood the needs and problems that pilots have and they never will. You must fly to understand the strange things that often happen in airplanes. What a night!

The next day the ORI hit. The dreaded Operational Readiness Inspection from SAC Headquarters that tested every base and every person for efficiency was upon us. For us aircrews these ORI's were always nuclear oriented but this one was SAC's first conventional ORI and they wanted to see if we could handle bombs other than nukes. We were thoroughly tested and then given a low level mission to fly around the islands. We were to drop a full load of bombs onto a rock off the southwest tip of Rota, an island just north of Guam.

Actually, the mission was a lot of fun. We toured the Marianas and waggled our wings at people fishing off the white beaches of truly remote islands. They watched us in obvious wonderment and little kids ran around waving and jumping up and down in the sand. Fifteen B-52 crews got to fly this mission and our crew was second across the target. We came in at five hundred feet above the water and popped up to drop from fifteen hundred feet to avoid the bomb blasts. Just before we popped up, I saw the rock and the bombs from the plane in front of us. I doubt many people have ever seen such a sight. The bombs walked toward the huge rock and, as the first one exploded, every bird on that rock took to the air in justified panic. What overkill, since only a few bombs could possibly hit the rock in the mile-long string of bomb blasts. We were graded for score from the center of our string of bombs and Terry was one of only two radar navigators to get credited with a "shack"—a direct hit. There was little left of the rock after the last B-52 passed. Well, it was practice!

A corollary to this ORI was the Biggs nuclear rotational force. They, too, were tested and when the Klaxon sounded for them, we all ran out of our barracks to watch eight B-52's start up and pretend to take off in the standard games SAC had us play. Jim Erbes, Jay Collier, and I watched the scramble from a rise about two hundred yards away, listening to the noise and watching the excitement. The crews all race to be first across the runway threshold on these exercises, pride being the driving force. After all, SAC's motto was, "Pride Is Our Profession."

Sixty-four jets were quickly started and immediately one bomber began moving. If he got onto the taxiway first, the others would have to give way. Jay pointed to the air cart, which was still hooked up near the bomber's rear landing gear truck. We were dumbstruck! The B-52 taxied forward and wrapped the airhose and then the cart itself around the wheels and it started to burn. He made it as far as the choke point in front of the runway before the fire trucks stopped him, but he had blocked all the other bombers! The firemen immediately put out the blaze but the Biggs guys flunked the ORI right there.

They deployed home right after that and, from then on, the B-52's at Andersen Air Force Base, Guam, were conventional only. We later discussed what General LeMay might have done to the pilot of that B-52 who taxied early. I'm certain he was boiled alive in a vat of hot oil.

Eventually, the party had to end. A couple of days later we were told to stay near the barracks and talk with no one. That really got the rumors flying! The rumor mill shifted into high gear and guys were even calling their wives back home to see if the Officers' Wives' Rumor Mill had anything. Nope. The next day we were ordered into combat! From that day, June 18, 1965, until the very last mission of the "Twelve Days of Christmas" in 1972, the B-52 played one of the most important roles in the Vietnam War. The war's symbol may have been the Huey helicopter but its great metaphor was the B-52.

Chapter Eight

Strategic Air Command's very first real live combat briefing was held in a large classroom. Thirty air crews, 180 men, plus four spares, listened carefully as staff colonels solemnly briefed the mission from maps and butcher paper balanced on makeshift easels. SAC Headquarters had planned the mission, which was fairly simple and straightforward. We would take off and climb to a cruising altitude of 30,000 feet in ten cells of three using colors for call signs. Our crew was Green Three, the third bomber in the third cell. Each cell would meet its cell of tankers on five aerial refueling tracks that extended southwest, down the South China Sea from off the northern tip of the Philippines. With bombs on board, we would not overfly land until coasting in over South Vietnam from Point Alpha, famous throughout the war as the primary clearance point into the war zone. The target lay in the jungle area of War Zone C, near the Michelin rubber plantation inside the Iron Triangle about thirty miles northwest of Saigon. After bomb release we were to climb to 45,000 feet and fly directly back to Guam.

The weatherman said we would have 100-knot headwinds at our cruising altitude. This only one of many great mistakes in the planning of the mission. The refueling tracks were supposed to be 50 miles apart and instead, SAC laid them out 25 miles apart. Also, there were no timing triangles or"ladders," usually used to make up or lose a bit of time in order to meet refueling and target timing requirements. Typhoon Dinah had just crossed the Philippines and was now in the South China Sea moving north toward Taiwan—and it changed the wind patterns. Instead of a 100-knot headwind, we had a 100-knot tailwind! And that resulted in everyone taking off ten minutes early to meet their timing requirements!

General Ohlke, the 3rd Air Division Commander, was more concerned about the timing at the Air Refueling Control Point, where we would meet our tankers, than the TOT, the Time-Over-Target. In his short pep talk he briefed us to"be on time" at the ARCP to meet the tankers—or everyone would be milling around above a typhoon at the same altitude in the dark! How correct he would be.

In every accident, whether it is a cut finger or a plane crash, a series of events leads to the point of unavoidable injury or worse. At any given time before the event, if, for example, the housewife puts the knife down to answer the phone, or if one minor mistake is recognized and corrected by the person in command of an operation, the chain of events may be blocked. How many accidents have NOT occurred because another distraction or a recognition of the impending problem changes the events about to occur? Another path is taken and disaster is unknowingly or inadvertently avoided. How many accidents in this world could be prevented if people only recognized they were heading for disaster? How many wars . . . ?

I recall something like seven contributing factors and one great unlikely error that led to the destruction of two B-52's and eight lives that night. I've relived the accident a thousand times and I'm certain that I could have done any of a hundred things that would have prevented it. Interfere with any one of those things in the chain leading to the disaster, and we might have blithely gone on flying through the night to our target with nothing amiss.

If only I had taken the plane off altitude hold and flown it higher by 60 feet! If only I had maneuvered the plane farther to the outside of the turn! If only I had backtalked to Jim Gehrig just once and told him to strap in before I relinquished control of the plane to him! If only the weatherman . . . If only the General . . . If only the SAC planners . . . If only a radar set had not failed . . . If only our cell leader had decided not to do a 360-degree turn . . .

If only I had decided instead to become a lawyer (ugh!) . . . If only another crew had been chosen to fly in our spot and us in theirs . . . If only . . .

I've spent most of my lifetime trying to figure this out. The survivor guilt feelings drove me to fly combat tour after combat tour, to be willing to sacrifice my own sweet body because I didn't die in that midair collision. Who knows what would have happened.

What if we had not crashed? The B-52 would have been glorified in its combat role while the people of America approved of kicking some butt in Vietnam instead of playing like pussycats. Had we not crashed maybe President Johnson would have said," Okay, tomorrow go to North Vietnam and destroy their war-making capability. And China and Russia, stay out or you might understand what our B-52's can really do!" Had he done that, the Vietnam War would not have happened the way it did and we would have ended the conflict in a couple of days. And don't ever let anyone tell you we couldn't have done it either! I was there from start to finish. I can't even talk of proposed targets. But, during the "Twelve Days of Christmas" of 1972, the B-52's actually ended the Vietnam War by destroying every strategic target in North Vietnam—after eight frustrating and deadly years of political indecision. And you've been told we lost the war! It was two long years after we left that Vietnam was given to the communists politically. Read the old newspapers of the day to see the truth because the history books have been changed.

A B-52 packs tremendous power if it is used properly. Instead of bombing supply depots, airfields, docks, railroad yards, bridges, petroleum storage, troop concentrations, infrastructure, etc., we were forced to go against smaller, nothing targets in a jungle where we couldn't see what we'd hit. This allowed the North Vietnamese to remain intact, to build upon their strategic targets for eight long years without even so much as harassment by our fighters. But that decision was kept tightly under control by Johnson and later by Nixon. If only . . . But it didn't happen that way, it happened the way it did. And here's how.

Air Force blue buses took us to Base Ops for a late-night snack and to pick up our in-flight box lunches. A photographer was supposed to fly with our crew to record SAC's first combat mission but he didn't show up and he's still alive today, probably unaware how close was his early end.

The bus dropped us off at our B-52 which was parked on the same hardstand that, four months earlier, had been ours upon arrival in Guam. Tropical nights can be incredibly dark, and we used flashlights to probe around the plane, working through the preflight checklist. The navigators crawled around and over the bombs in the bomb bay, pulling pins and checking every bomb for fusing, safety delay, and security.

An Aircrew Information File item ordered everyone to release and resnap the new disconnect rings on both risers of every parachute at least five times before each mission for ten missions until all of them worked without binding. This problem should have been taken care of by the parachute shop. It was their job! Throughout my career I saw this sort of thing, where a few people worked harder to avoid work than to just do the job right the first time! What I loved most about military pilots was that they never shirked.

We secured, started the engines, performed the checklist, and waited. Including spares, thirty-four bombers somehow got into the correct lineup for takeoff. To me, it appeared as confusing as a herd of cattle wandering around in the dark, but we got in line and worked our way toward the runway.

The first B-52 rolled across the threshold exactly on the BBC hack at 3:00 a.m. Its dark shape plunged down the runway with billowing black smoke from its engines roiling behind it, obscuring everything. The high-pitched screech of 264 more idling jet engines was drowned by the throaty roar of that first bomber as it accelerated down the runway slope. The noise of its eight jets drifted back to us, ninth in line. By the time it reached takeoff speed at the far end of the runway, the next bomber began its takeoff roll. It, too, belched black smoke with a reverberation so deafening that it could be heard all over the island. And, after it, another bomber rolled. And soon, another cell.

Green Leader waited an extra two minutes for cell separation and then he rolled. A minute later all I could see of him was a flashing red beacon as he disappeared into his own smoke over the cliff and out across the ocean. Green Two, the bomber in front of us, took the runway pushing his engines to full power, and his roar was louder than all the rest. Within a few seconds the sound waves were deadened in the roiling violence of turbulence behind his screaming jet engines.

Then it was our turn. Terry called out ten seconds and counted down from five. At zero we crossed the hold line and Jim pushed the throttles about halfway forward until he was nearly lined up on the runway. He pushed them full forward and told me the throttles were mine as he concentrated on the takeoff. I held them, locking full forward as the thrust behind us shot our giant B-52 down the initial dip in the Andersen runway. Our wings bucked in the turbulence left behind by the other departing bombers. The blackness was as dark as the pit of the Marianas Trench and I kept my eyes glued to the red, glowing engine instruments and called for water injection for extra thrust. Without looking into the cockpit, Jim reached down and flipped the water injection switch and the engines screeched like banshees with water pouring into the jet compressors even faster than fuel into the jet burner cans.

In seconds the airspeed indicator came off the peg at 60 knots and a small dip in the runway bounced us slightly. We rocked up and down, constantly, gradually, slowly picking up speed. We were heavy. Twenty-seven 1,000-pound bombs were tucked in the bomb bay and another twenty-four 750-pounders hung on racks under the wings. Three hundred ten thousand pounds of jet fuel filled the wings and fuselage tanks along with 10,000 pounds of water injection that would be completely devoured within two minutes.

We bounced again and Terry called the line speed check—our acceleration was proper. We were committed to the takeoff now and could not stop in the mile of remaining runway even in an emergency. At the end of the runway was a cliff that dropped 600 feet to the black sea. At 100 knots the tires began to rattle like they wanted to throw their tread in protest against the heavy weight and speed. It shook the plane like a rat in the jaws of a giant Doberman.

The acceleration above 100 knots was sluggish, and even the ORI, with a full load of bombs, had not weighed down our B-52's like this fully loaded combat mission. This was a first! The B-52 was designed for a nuclear role and carrying this extra weight of conventional bombs was an afterthought. I stole a peek outside to see the runway end lights approaching fast. We were nowhere near unstick speed and I rocked my neck forward urging the huge bomber to go faster.

I waited, willing this overweight beast into the air. The wheels bounced us hard now, jolting the plane and sending terrible shudders through its frame.

There's the end of the runway, I thought, checking the airspeed with only a few knots to go. "Okay, Unstick, NOW!" I said, relieved. Jim eased the yoke back and the giant ceased its vibrations and became airborne. The wings grabbed at the humid, tropical air and lifted us smoothly into a deep blackness. Underneath, the cliff sped by and I felt, more than saw, the ocean six hundred feet below. We did not climb, accelerating instead straight ahead. My eyes remained on the instruments as the airspeed continued to increase.

Jim also kept his eyes inside the cockpit, now flying on instruments. He reached forward and lifted the landing gear handle. Far to the rear, the hydraulic systems came on line to hoist up the four large landing gear trucks and the two spindly outrigger gears near the wing tips.

When the gear doors indicated closed, Jim called, "Flaps, fifteen." I raised the flap lever to the next detent and he clicked in trim to compensate for the shift in the flap setting. It felt like we would sink into the sea—but the altitude held. We ignored our flying-by-the-seat-of-our-pants feelings and continued flying on instruments. "Flaps up," he said, and their whine echoed through the structure of the plane until they locked up full.

Suddenly, one at a time, the engines seemed to flame out. But it was the water injection, spent. Again I glanced outside the cockpit. Two red rotating beacons of the B-52's ahead of us arced left across the windscreen, slightly high, turning on course for Vietnam. We rolled left and followed them. At three thousand feet we popped through the thin layer of puffball clouds that constantly floated across the Western Pacific and transposed into a sphere of a hundred billion pinpoints of light. The only place I'd ever seen so many stars was at night in the Polar Zone. Jim reached behind the throttle quadrant and turned on the autopilot, then sat back to relax. We were on our way. To combat.

I pulled out my fuel log and began the task of writing down all the readings in our fuel tanks. My eyes constantly strayed around the cockpit, glancing for signs of an impending engine failure and, once again, checking the fuel system. I had never had a single problem with the alternators or electrical system on a B-52. It was time for sleep, and we pilots are no different from anyone else. It was, after all, 3:30 a.m. The pre-mission excitement was over and, except for the refueling and the bomb run, only boredom lay ahead and boredom in anything is an inducement to sleep. Unfortunately I could only border on sleep.

Although the mission required radio silence until after bomb release, someone was talking on one of our radios. I perked up for a moment. Green Leader had lost his attack radar and needed to change positions with Green Two. The radar navigator in Green Leader had several backup ways to drop his bombs by flying directly behind the guy in front and using timing. So, Green Leader flew to the side and changed positions with number two. No problem.

I was too sleepy to pay close attention. This was no big deal, Green Two would be our new leader and would retain his call sign. We all knew who was where. One glance at Jim and we both understood where everybody was located and we both went back into our dream world. We kept station a mile behind the second man in our cell and 500 feet above him. But apparently the Russians in the "trawler" knew what we were up to and they relayed the first of many messages to their friends in Hanoi.

I was tired now. We'd been up since early morning the day before, unable to sleep because of the combat rumors. Somewhere, inside my normal brain functioning, something kept telling me that this was simply another goat roping, game playing, harassment of aircrews designed, diabolically, by SAC to keep us on our toes. We weren't really going to war, it was just another SAC exercise to show the force. Soon, we would be recalled and return to base with tanks empty and bombs still on the racks. I suppose this is what repetitive training does to the mind, so when actual combat arrives, it is already routine.

I gave the gunner an oxygen check, logged another fuel chart, and had another half hour to stare into the blackness with only the red rotating beacons of the bombers in front of us to break the monotony. A translucent glow emanated from their skins as if they were alive, like huge silver beasts that cruised the skies searching for prey.

I remembered a friend in pilot training who had been a navigator and one night he got up and walked around the plane to find that both pilots were asleep. He figured they knew what they were doing and went back to his seat. A while later he checked again and they were still asleep but the plane was on course and altitude and he once again figured they knew what they were doing, this time in their sleep. He applied for pilot training shortly after that.

On an all-night flight, one pilot will cat-nap while

the other kind of watches things, even dozing a bit. Then they switch so the other can get some sleep. We learned this quickly on our Chrome Dome missions. I've done it many times. If the plane starts jerking around or if an engine blows up, you are going to know it soon enough and you'll be wide awake with all your adrenaline pumping. At 30,000 feet over the Western Pacific, what can you run into, a Canadian goose?

Three and a half hours into the flight we approached the aerial refueling rendezvous where the tankers from Kadena would fill our tanks. We passed north of the Philippines and turned southwest for the Aerial Refueling Control Point, the ARCP. I got out of my seat and went downstairs to stretch my legs and chat with the navigators about how early we were because of the typhoon. The navigators were busy as hell and angry that the weatherman had given us winds that were two hundred knots off, which caused us to be nine minutes early for the rendezvous. I'm certain every navigator in our force was thinking of the disaster of navigation in the World War II bombing raid on the Ploesti Oil Fields in Romania.

While I was out of the seat, there was a conversation among the pilots in our cell about doing a 360-degree turn to lose the nine minutes. When I crawled back into my seat, Jim jumped up all excited about something and ran downstairs to take his nervous pre-refueling leak. In hindsight, I realized the 360 was what upset him. I woke the gunner up, gave him an oxygen check, and told him we were about to begin refueling. He didn't answer the first time and I had to waggle the rudders. Meanwhile, I strapped into my para-chute and seat harness. I think the gunner went back to sleep.

Suddenly, the lead B-52 rolled into a 30-degree left turn and number two followed him!

"Hey Radar," I said to Terry, "What are they doing, a 360?"

"Rog," he answered, "where were you?"

"Out of my seat, I called it." But navigators rarely listened to pilot chatter.

I was quite upset but rolled the autopilot knob into a 30-degree bank and followed our cell leader. I quickly figured that if they did a standard-rate 360, it would take eight minutes and describe a 25-nautical-mile diameter circle. With refueling tracks 25 miles apart and cells following each other at four minutes—half a turn of eight minutes is four minutes—it did not take a genius to figure out that we might run into someone head on if they were flying up the track just south of ours.

"Radar," I said to Terry, "if there's another cell coming up the track south of us we're going to meet them head on!"

"That's right, Copilot," he said, "keep your eyes open!"

"Rog!"

"What the hell are they doing, a 360?" Jim hollered as he jumped back into his seat, angry. He took control of the airplane and maneuvered us just outside the other B-52's in the turn.

I re-cinched my parachute straps, rechecked my seat

belt, and made doubly certain the ejection seat pins were removed. I peered out into the blackness above the typhoon, which crackled with lightning flashes. I thought the chances of having a head-on collision over the vast South China Sea were extremely remote. It would probably be one of those moments of sheer terror they talked about as we passed each other in the night sky without even a sighting. The stars above spread out into the Milky Way like I'd only seen above the North Pole. The sky had been cleaned by the typhoon, and there were no distracting lights to block the view of any of the billions of stars.

"WE GOT BEACONS AT FOUR MILES AND CLOSING FAST!" Terry shouted.

I studied the sky ahead. There! Directly in front of us was a small light that did not move across the windscreen, an indication that we were flying directly toward something. Then, I saw three lights distinctly, two in my peripheral vision but not far from the center of where I was looking. One light was above and to the left of the first light's sighting and the other was down and to the right of the first light. The two outside lights diverged slowly across the wind-screen away from the converging light in the middle.

With dumbstruck amazement I stared at the center light as it split into two lights, apparently the wing tip lights of another aircraft. My mind, now alarmed, accelerated, expanding time into another dimension where microseconds, one thousandth of a second, seemed to take minutes.

The scene became weird and everything moved in extreme slow motion. Even as I write this, it is as vivid as the night it occurred.

"WE'RE ON A COLLISION COURSE! WE'RE GO-ING DOWN!" Jim shouted over the radio.

I've spent years trying to analyze exactly what he meant. Was he trying to dive below the bomber coming at us? Did he know we were probably going down, meaning, he knew we were going to crash? Out of the corner of my eye I saw him leaning slightly forward—and he was looking up and to the left. After all these years, I'm now certain he had seen the bomber on our left and knew that we would have a near miss—that it would be close but that we would miss. Time was passing for me in microseconds and I remember Jim began to push over into a slight dive. He was looking at the wrong plane. But at the time I didn't know it.

Our closing speed was 1058 miles per hour, each bomber flying at 450 knots, and yet, to me, the episode was taking hours to occur. We were committed and I wanted desperately to grab the yoke and jerk it back into my lap but there was no way to counter Jim's radio call or to ana-lyze the situation further, argue it out or do anything else. (Besides, all I've discussed here took place in about five sec-onds.)

The quickness of the human mind in extremely stress-ful situations is remarkable. We came together faster than a rifle bullet and I watched in fascinated amazement as that B-52 flew straight into our cockpit! Its wing-tip lights now

spread apart, revealing a great, gray shadow that was un-
mistakably another B-52. My mind accepted the fact that
it would hit us directly head on. There was no longer any
doubt about it. The 3,000-gallon drop tank that hung under
its right wing grew large in front of me. It was a nightmare!
I remember distinctly having the time to think, "This is a
surreal dream!" I was watching myself about to die in slow
motion and there was nothing I could do about it. That
drop tank was going to hit me right in the face.

I went through all the human emotions in the matter of
a single second. Like someone dealing with terminal cancer
over a lengthy period of time, I denied, then was angry,
then was accepting of death and became peaceful. I resigned myself to it, to a smashing death—quick, hard, clean,
zap, dead! From that split-second forth, I became the only
person in the entire history of the planet (other than drug
users) to know what it is like to fly into something at such a
high speed, because nobody else has ever lived through an
experience like this. It was the very beginning of my own
death, and it was absolutely fascinating to watch.

Their drop tank grew so large in front of me that I knew
it was only a matter of a few feet, and at a closing speed of
1540 feet per second! Many times since this "incident," I've
stood in front of a B-52 parked on the ground and tried
to estimate how far away the drop tank really was when
I accepted death by smashing, and I always guessed the
distance to be less than 100 feet. Only during the writing
of this book did I come to verify that this was actually so.

Gene Crissey, the radar navigator on Yellow Three, the plane that was up and to our left, told me recently that they picked us up at 14 nautical miles on their radar and that Yellow Two went into a steep dive as quickly as he could. We picked their cell up at only four nautical miles on Terry's radar. I saw them about two or three miles out and we simply did not have the time to analyze the situation. Regardless, the B-52 is very slow to respond to any flight control input and neither of us could have changed the fact that we would hit each other—head on.

Somehow, the pilot of the other bomber was diving his plane in a desperate attempt to avoid us. His drop tank slowly, slowly (at over 1000 miles per hour) dropped away from our wind-screen and disappeared under our nose. The gray leviathan, much larger than anything that had ever flown or even cruised the ocean depths, glided ever so slowly past my window. Slowly, like watching a whale swim by, the six-story tail drifted past as in a dream and I thought, "Whew! We missed!"

Then, in a micro-heartbeat, I realized that I was wrong.

In that short span of time, maybe one thirtieth of a second, my mind reasoned that, in fact, if their drop tank was about to enter our cockpit, then our drop tank would hit their vertical stabilizer, their tail! I braced for the impact, looking straight ahead, knowing it would be bad—and I waited, an eternity.

The impact itself jarred our plane about the same as if we'd driven a car over a large pothole in the road going about thirty miles per hour. Our right wing, in the drop tank area, impacted the base of their tail, the thousand-mile-an-hour speed slicing through rather than crunching, like two cars head on. Our cockpit went totally black and for a moment I waited for death. It would be quick and it didn't seem like it would be painful.

Some time later, there was an explosion—the brightest thing I'd ever seen then, or ever seen to this day. Of course, I was at the center of it. The explosion was totally consuming, a blinding orange. Trailing B-52 cells saw the explosion as far away as two hundred miles. The bright orange quickly dissipated and was replaced again by a complete blackness. I was blind. I was alive, but how could I fly this jet bomber blind? I glanced toward Jim and my vision began to return but I could see only as far as the throttles. I was not really blind! Just blinded by the explosion.

Immediately, I grabbed the yoke to feel the plane and peered over it to see if I could even see any flight instruments. I could not see any of them in the blackout. All my senses told me to turn about 90 degrees left and head for Clark Air Force Base in the Philippines, north of Manila. We seemed to be flying but I knew that at the least, our wingtip was missing. I did not know at the time that our entire right wing had blown off! I thought if we could only keep her airborne until we can make it to Clark . . . maybe. Let's try! But that fatal thinking has probably killed more pilots than any other cause. Never stay with a fatally crippled airplane that is out of control! But I wasn't even certain at the time if we were out of control.

We hear stories about pilots guiding their disabled aircraft away from school yards and hospitals. This is a myth perpetuated by those who do not understand flying. When it happens, there is no time to think and sort these things out in a plane that is going down!

A short time later, how long I will never know since I may still have been living in a distorted time frame, my vision recovered enough to see the outline of the dashboard against a lightning flash from Typhoon Dinah, below us. "Great!" I thought, "Now I can find out which way is up from the attitude indicator!"

But it was not to be! Just as I leaned forward to peek at the attitude indicator somebody ejected and it fogged up the cockpit and again turned everything black. I had no way of knowing, until later, that we were going straight down. The right wing had exploded and blew away because it is one gigantic fuel tank.

The smell of death entered my nostrils and I could not identify it as the cordite from someone's ejection seat until much later. The airplane now smelled of death. It was dying.

There comes a time in the mind of every pilot who ever ejected when he knows, "It's time to jettison the airplane! Those who hesitate, die!" It is usually a once-in-a-lifetime event so I wanted to do it correctly. I bolted to the ejection position, head hard against the headrest, butt against the parachute, back straight, legs tucked back, hands on the armrest ejection handles. I was ready.

I pulled up on both handles—but only the left handle came up and seated into position. I squeezed the left ejection trigger and waited an eternity for the 15 g's to shoot me out of the cockpit on a howitzer shell. Soon I would be flung into the night air above the typhoon. But nothing happened!

I squeezed the left trigger again, and again, but still, nothing! I jerked upward on the right handle as hard as I could pull with both hands. It was welded down and there was no time remaining to check the pins that I already had double checked earlier! That handle was not going to rotate! I cursed the people who were supposed to take care of these things and squeezed the left trigger one more time. Nothing!

There was one option. Inside the armrests are two more handles, one to release the survival kit and the other to release the parachute from the seat, as it was an "integrated" harness. I could then get up from the seat with only the parachute and manually bail out of one of the navigator's hatches downstairs. I would be without my life raft and survival kit. At the time no one had ever successfully bailed out of a B-52 manually and lived to tell the story! But there was no time left!

I looked down at that ejection handle, it lay hard in my left hand. I decided to give it one more try and then accept death. I jerked once more and the son of a bitch fired when

I didn't expect it! My head was down and out of position with a five-pound helmet sitting on it! The force of the ejection would tear my head off.

Chapter Nine

The ejection seat accelerated upward with more force than a rocket. It was a 105mm howitzer shell! I watched the dashboard slowly fall away, and the hatch descended toward me. Then I was blasted in the face with a wind so powerful that ten typhoons would have seemed like a gentle afternoon breeze. Suddenly, the B-52 exploded! A microsecond more and I would have been blown to bits! Two tremendous explosions, one immediately following the other, hit me with a forceful Whump! Whump! And a half-second later another, smaller explosion split the night with a concussion that sent something flying into my left calf, pulverizing the central muscle. (Will somebody please explain this to the VA? They still don't believe I was ever in a crash!)

The parachute opened with a mild shock and I was

suspended, high in the night sky, above the most startling scene I've ever imagined. Rome was burning below me on the ocean surface. The entire world was afire, like Dante's inferno, on the South China Sea!

Fascinated, I stared dumbly at the flames. Pockets of fire spread for miles, lighting up the inside of the typhoon with an eerie glow of Halloween oranges and blacks. Fear and panic overcame me, and I had to consciously fight off both in order to survive! I wanted to scream and release myself to the panic, to let it go, a natural human instinct. But I knew I'd die if I let panic eat my soul. Fight panic! Fight panic! I had to convince myself of this every single second.

It seemed I was in a dream world, conscious and aware but with a distorted sense of time. My mind was still at 30,000 feet, where it thought I might die of hypoxia. I fumbled with the "green apple" on the emergency oxygen bottle attached to one of the parachute risers. My helmet was still on my head and the oxygen mask was still attached. But I could NOT breathe! If I took off the helmet I'd die of hypoxia, and still I could not breathe. PANIC! Fight panic! Fight panic! I yanked and jerked on that green apple but could not get oxygen to flow. Oh God! I'm going to suffocate! I'm going to die right here in this parachute!

I consciously forced myself to calm down. To think rationally. And I realized that if my parachute had opened automatically, then I must be below 14,000 feet, where the air was heavier. I released the oxygen mask. How simple! I could breathe. What a relief. The air was cool and fresh and clean and lifesaving and I gulped it like there was never going to be enough. I let my mask dangle over my left cheek and looked down again at the sea.

The ocean burned. I wanted to dream and watch the spectacle but I needed to think. Mae West! Open the Mae West! Pull the lanyard and they will open automatically. Then you won't have that to worry about when you hit the water. I pulled both lanyards and both Mae West's fell out of their pouches and fell flat like puppy dogs' ears. They did not inflate! The people who were supposed to keep these things in working order had not checked the CO_2 cylinders! No problem though, I could blow them up by mouth. But before I got the chance to do it I was distracted.

The energy that drives a typhoon, a hurricane, is heat. The sun stirs the bowels of the ocean, generating swirls and winds that, once begun, continue to build until heat is released in giant thunderstorms, each with the power of a nuclear bomb!

Directly below me, the flames from a half-million pounds of burning jet fuel had created a thunderstorm of their own. A mushroom cloud built and boiled up toward me like a roaring freight train. I estimated this inferno of boiling heat cloud climbed toward me at 20,000 feet per minute! I'd never seen or ever heard of a building thunderstorm climbing anywhere near that fast, but with jet fuel burning directly below me and with the heat generated by the typhoon . . . when it reached me it would tear apart my flimsy parachute and drop me into the sea like Icarus with his melted waxen wings. This was truly hell itself! The lake of fire, the River Styx! And I had only a bit of thin spun nylon to protect myself.

Panic! Panic! Fight panic! Fight panic! Think, you idiot! Think! In a matter of seconds, I would be eaten by that mushroom non-nuclear cloud, to be devoured and spit out to fall eternally in a death scream to Hell! Fight panic!

Slip the parachute! Slip the parachute! Slip it sideways, away from the boiling, roiling hell-cloud. I reached up and pulled on two of the four risers, with no time to make a "four-line cut," as the Air Force had taught us for maneuvering. I jerked down hard on the risers and the parachute slipped sideways, skidding across the boiling sky. The mushroom cloud flashed upward beside me. I felt the breeze and it buffeted the parachute but I was safe from the grip of that monster. But there were other, even more threatening monsters all around on that dark night.

When I let go of the risers, the parachute swung back. And it kept swinging. Then it swung farther forward, and then farther! Then back. Then forward again and back! Each time the amplitude got larger! What was happening? I was a child sitting on a swing and my dad was trying to push me over the top. Oh God! Panic again! Fight panic! I looked down upon the parachute and saw the fires beginning to bum out below me. I was past the horizontal! The gods in that thunderstorm wanted to flip me over into the bowl of my own parachute! They wanted me dead! Fight panic!

For some long-forgotten reason, a strange thought came into my frightened mind. From my studies of university physics, the Law of Conservation of Angular Momentum entered my brain—one more swing and I'd be wrapped in a death shroud of parachute cloth—I quickly pulled my survival kit release handle, and a bright yellow life raft burst from the survival kit strapped to my butt. It inflated and fell on its lanyard about 50 feet below me. The survival kit was attached to the lanyard about 30 feet down and, together, they halted the oscillation. I hung directly below the parachute, elated. Again I had beaten the gods of nature with one of nature's own laws. The parachute remained stable with the long moment arm of the raft and survival kit.

The fires below were almost burned out. Soon it would be as black as Tobin's goat once again and I would not be able to determine which way was up or how near the sea I was. Hell, now in a dark place! I looked around, twisting my sore neck to see if I was the only one hanging in a parachute, the only one alive. There! Behind me, about a half-mile away, was another parachute, white with Day-Glo orange panels. Someone else made it! I wondered who it was and I reached up to twist the risers in opposite directions in order to turn the parachute so I could see the other survivor. It was easy, we practiced this in survival school. But it didn't work the way they taught us!

The parachute rotated slowly until I faced the other survivor, and I let the parachute go when it turned the correct amount. I shouted at him. But the parachute itself had other intentions. It kept rotating! I grabbed at the risers, twisting them in the opposite direction to stop the rotation but it didn't stop! I looked up and saw that the parachute was getting smaller with each rotation. Holy Jesus! It was going to twist itself into a tiny ball and I would fall to my death just as I might have before! Oh no! Panic! Panic! Fight panic! Fight panic!

I pulled tighter against the rotation, and the twisting finally slowed and stopped and began to spin slowly the other way. Soon, I would be in the same predicament but in the other direction. You devils of the air are diabolical! You are putting me through the ordeal of fire and water with a twist! The Air! As the parachute unwound, I controlled the spin with jerks, and at the bottom, before it twisted back up the other way, I "popped" the risers and the parachute stabilized. I decided that if I spent a year in that parachute, there was no way I was going to screw around with it again until it safely deposited me in the water. I could not, at that time, believe it had two more lethal tricks to play!

Oh, dear sweet God, when I hit the water all hell will break loose! Keep me here, Lord, temporarily safe in the cradle of this damned parachute, high here in the dark sky. Dear God, I'll live out the rest of my life just hanging here, just don't, please don't, let me down into that raging sea! Oh, please! Please!

The fires were completely burned out, and the sky was dark once again. An occasional flash of lightning lit up both the sky and the sea and I successfully fought off panic for one more minute.

What would happen when I landed? Ha! There was a misnomer! The waves below frothed with whitecaps and blowing seawater. I'd be lucky to even crawl into my life raft. The sea was much closer and it seemed to glow in a frothy, turquoise green. I did not know why it emitted this light, unless the typhoon had stirred up small plankton that glowed when they were agitated. Now, I could plainly see the waves foaming, and I wanted desperately to hang in the parachute until someone rescued me. But I had to face the prospect of adapting to the sea, I could not wish myself to hang in the parachute forever. Any second now! I'm going to hit those waves and it will be like jumping into a boiling volcano!

Feet together, eyes on the horizon, wait—keep your knees bent, wait, wait damn it! Keep looking at the horizon! Peek down. Oh God! It's close! Panic! Fight panic! Look at the horizon, don't panic! Easy now.

I hit a wave, went in up to my waist, and was instantly jerked sideways. Now, instead of falling, I was water-skiing behind the fastest motorboat in the world, my parachute! Caught by the wind, it towed me through the waves with incredible speed. The parachute twisted in the water, turning me face down and forcing huge amounts of salt water down my throat. I rolled and gulped a quick breath of spray and air before it twisted again. Damn this parachute! I spread my legs to try and stabilize, and it worked! But I was face down again, swallowing water. Somehow, I twisted and held my legs apart to stabilize upright. There was a true devil in that parachute!

I felt for the release clips in front of my collarbones and unhooked both covers; the pull-rings popped out. I pulled. Nothing! I jerked hard and still could not release the risers. The parachute continued to drag me through the waves at breakneck speed. I put both thumbs through the ring on the right riser and jerked as hard as I could, and still, nothing! I wondered if I would ski in this manner all the way to Taiwan, but it was a sick fantasy, a bad joke. I was already exhausted and just wanted to sit in the raft for a moment and rest. I cursed the people in the parachute shop who were supposed to maintain all this stuff. I distinctly remember thinking about the Aircrew Information File item that had us aircrews doing their work for them on this flight. We should not have gone into the air with defective equipment, especially when they probably spent most of their time at the beach, like us. They'd had four months to fix these things!

Damn, I was mad. With the determination to overcome the devil who rules these things, I jerked the right release ring with all my might and it gave way. One side of the parachute flipped away like a great bullwhip, and I stopped dead in the water. I thought for a moment that I might make it yet. In a rare moment, free of panic, I swam to the life raft and pulled it underneath me and was in. Then I turned over and sat upright, dazed with the situation facing me.

Another dimension now captivated my being: giant waves. I floated up, then down, then up, then down, skiing down the slope of each wave in a great monotony. Up, then down. Never ending, vertically pendulous, never changing. I was in the ocean! And I was alive!

The survival kit bobbed alongside the raft and I towed it into the tiny cockpit that was now my little world, the interior of the life raft. The air bladder was about eight inches in diameter, slightly larger at my back than at my feet where the raft narrowed. I fit perfectly into the thing with my knees raised. Inside, it was about two feet long and a foot-and-one-half wide, a very small bathtub.

I balanced the survival kit on my lap and it overflowed the life raft. A black rubber cover appeared liquid in the water that constantly washed over it. A tough, waterproof zipper crossed it diagonally and I pulled at it to open the kit but, like everything else, it didn't work. The zipper would not pull. I thought I had lost all my strength. If I could not open a simple, waterproof zipper with what strength I had remaining, then . . .

Need always overcomes obstacle. Inside a pouch on my inner left thigh was an orange switchblade survival knife, which I removed. I unwound the yard-long length of fine nylon cord that tied it to a grommet in the pouch. It had a rounded, parachute-hook blade open so as to make the "four-line cut" to guide the parachute and make it stable. I did not have time in the air to analyze and use it. I flipped open the switchblade, cut the zipper out of the kit, and carefully returned the knife to its pouch with only the hook blade open. That is the way it is customarily stowed, an old habit that I would soon find can actually be a fatal mistake.

The survival kit was packed with a wondrous assortment of things to keep a downed pilot alive—in the Arctic. At first, I was like a kid in a candy shop. Wow! Here's a little .22 "Hornet" rifle that came in two parts, a barrel about 18 inches long that screwed into the breech and stock of the same length. I quickly assembled it; the stock was simply quarter-inch steel tubing with a small pad on the end. I was amazed at its simplicity and functionality. Neat. Now, what would I do with it? Shoot a polar bear?

I don't know why, but I held the rifle over the side of the raft and dropped it into the sea, stock first. It fell into the waves with a sucking sound, "thrup," and was gone forever.

Next, I found a foot-square, fiberglass thing about one or two inches thick that had a wing nut on one side exactly in the middle. Written on it was something like, "one each, Arctic sleeping bag," and I truly wondered how they had stuffed a whole sleeping bag into this tiny space. I twisted the wing nut but it didn't budge, typical of everything so far. Normally, for my size, I was a very strong guy, and yet I wondered if I had lost all my strength.

I twisted the wing nut harder, wishing I had a pair of pliers but it was no use, the wing nut was frozen and I didn't need an Arctic survival sleeping bag anyway. It was summer and I was in the South China Sea. At the top of the next large wave I laid it on the water and watched it ski, faster than the raft, down to the bottom of the trough and disappear into the sea. Another fine piece of American technology down the drain—literally.

I don't know how they fit so many things into that tiny kit, but inside was a huge pair of socks and a ski mask, all of gray wool. Excellent for hunting or Arctic wear, but I was in a tropical south sea. I realized I was really cold and thought of taking off my helmet to try out the ski mask but felt ridiculous, even alone. I actually thought of how foolish I would feel if they found me dead, floating around wearing a ski mask in the South China Sea, in summer with a perfectly good helmet sitting in my lap. I was mentally transferring into another world and didn't yet know it. We all do silly things in times of great stress. I stuffed these items at my side and, for some reason, tied myself to the raft with a piece of parachute cord. That act would later save my life.

Out came an Arctic survival book with paintings of flowers and plants from the tundra that were edible and others that were bad or poisonous. It described how to quickly build an ice house—an igloo—and how to skin a seal. I fumbled through the kit for something useful in a tropical sea and could find nothing of value! What were those parachute shop boys doing? Spending too much time at the beach or the South Seas Club, or drinking too much beer. I was getting really pissed off.

There was not a thing in the entire kit that I could use, not even a flashlight or especially the strobe light flasher or even a flare. Where was the survival radio? Where were these things? At the rear of the survival kit I noticed broken flanges where all the communication gear had probably been tucked. The compartment was gone, broken off in the ejection! The only communication equipment I had was a survival mirror.

Although it was still as dark as the pits of Hell, there seemed to be enough light to see across the raging waves when I reached the top of a swell. The swells were about 25 feet high, and it took ten seconds or so to rise to the top, another ten seconds to drop to the bottom, and another ten to go to the top again. Monotony, seasickness, vomiting, retching. It just didn't stop, the rise and fall. I was nothing but a leaf, floating in a mighty sea that thought nothing of dashing me under a crashing wave to the bottom. A faint glow emanated through the clouds from the east, and it gave me a semblance of direction.

Of all the strange things I'd seen this night, one of the strangest lay about half a mile due north of me. There, struggling through the waves, was a large black ship with orange trim! What the hell? I'd never been on an ocean-going ship before and thought I might be dreaming . . . or dead already. It took several seconds to adjust to the fact that there really was a ship plowing through the waves only a short distance away! I shouted into the wind. My yelling went unheard in the screaming wind and I felt stupid.

I scrambled again through the kit, looking frantically for something I could signal with—nothing. Panic! He's going to get away! Panic! Fight panic! Don't panic! I glanced up again and now knew for certain that I was hallucinating because what I saw then was even stranger.

The black and orange ship was heading generally west just north of me. Coming south on a line about half a mile west from me was a Disneyland fantasy ocean liner, a princess all dressed in white! The princess was about to crash into the side of the black ship just like the Guamanian couple crashed into the side of the sailors' Guam Bomb! Now I knew it was an hallucinatory dream because it was simply unbelievable. They, too, were going to collide! It had to be a dream, a throwback to the Guam car crash. My mind—was this what minds do to people when they are about to die? To play games with our minds using the only deaths we'd ever witnessed?

Still, I searched for a flare. None! Then I sat back in the life raft to just watch the scene unfold for a minute. Slipping down into the swells, I could not see anything but walls of water on all sides, but when I was on top of a wave I could see for a couple of miles, and I thought of the irony. At this one location in the whole world, only an hour and 30,000 feet separating them, two warplanes and two ships collide! If the ships were real then maybe there would be a quick rescue operation. Then again, maybe all the people on those ships would fight me for my little raft!

Down again into the depths of the water troughs. Up again to view the world for a few seconds. The ships! They missed! But it didn't matter, I was hallucinating and it just didn't matter. Half a mile to the west, what was that? A flare! Someone else is alive and shot a pencil flare into the sky! Sweet Jesus, a flare! They'll see it and save us! Another flare! And another!

Wait! The White Princess is going to run over the guy who shot the flare! It was so close that I could see the lacy railing on the decks, but there were no people out on deck in this storm. Wow! Another flare right beside the White Princess! That survivor nearly got himself run over! The ship wasn't even slowing down! Christ, they didn't see the flares. The person driving the ship was asleep or drinking coffee and just plowing through the waves. I'll bet he didn't see the Halloween ship either.

Down again. And up again. Just before I lost my balance I caught a glimpse of the foot end of my life raft. It was as floppy as my Mae West! What? Why? Holy, Sweet Je . . . ! I was dumped over into the water by the top of a wave and immediately went under. Above me was a faint glow of light. I was going down fast, being dragged under by a great weight. No more life raft! The survival kit. It was dragging me down. I couldn't breathe! I was going to die after all!

I reached up for the little ball of life raft, and my left arm dragged against the risers of the parachute! SHOCK! How stupid of me! I forgot to disconnect the parachute from my body and it was going to be the last mistake I'd ever make. And after all this surviving already. In training didn't they say that a wet parachute could soak up a ton of water in a matter of minutes? In seconds I would drown, but there might be a chance.

I jerked out my orange survival knife and grabbed a fistful of risers. With the hook blade I cut risers one at a time but it was too slow, there was not time . . . I flipped open the switchblade and, pulling on a handful of risers, I slashed and sliced my way through, cutting risers and fingers. It didn't matter anymore. I had seconds left. The will to breathe is all-powerful, slightly stronger than my sex drive, and I cut and sliced everything. I still carry small scars on my fingers.

Suddenly, I surfaced! Gasp! A few feet away, floating like a streak of yellow paint in the water, was my life raft. Thank God I'd tied myself to the raft earlier. I grabbed it and wadded it up underneath my arms. It was about the size of a basketball. I held on and gasped for breath, thankful once again for still being alive.

How I wanted to live! Now I was angry again and the anger gave me strength. The idiots at SAC Headquarters who planned this mission should be shot for stupidity. The bastards in the Parachute Shop and Personal Equipment should be jailed for life for laziness, negligence, and malfeasance, I swore. I shouted and I vowed to kill someone if I could only get a chance to get my hands on them! Adrenaline swam through my veins and gave me even more strength. I grabbed the inflation stem on the life raft and shoved it into my mouth. The outer stem moved forward and I blew into it. Nobody had ever told me that was how you were supposed to manually blow up a life raft because I'd never had any training on this. We were taught how to survive only in the Arctic.

I gleefully gasped for air and filled my raft with every breath. I'd beaten the devils of the sea once again! Ever so slowly the life raft filled with the air from my lungs that also gave me life. I screwed down the stem and it held and I crawled once again into the raft. The sun was on the horizon and it was light. The water was a dark green with white froth at the top of the waves.

The survival kit and all its useless contents were gone. But I was still alive and I had my .38-caliber service revolver, the Mae West's, and the white nylon cord that I tied myself to the life raft with. I blew into the Mae West's, filled them, and clipped them together in front of my chest. Then I surveyed what I had remaining.

My mother had sent me a care package with a large bag of M&M's that I'd put into one lower flight suit pocket. But the zipper was open and it was gone! Blown out in the ejection most likely. I checked my jacket and found that all my zippers were open. Everything personal was missing. It is the little things that cause despair during survival, and I became despondent for a while.

Except inside the reef at Tarague Beach, I'd never been in the sea before. I had no idea how dangerous the sea could be, how treacherous in so many ways. It is even less forgiving than the air. Now I had nothing to help me survive. I could only wait for a rescue. For the first time since infancy, I was totally dependent upon someone else and all I could do was sit and wait.

There were no ships, they had gone. Or were they even real in the first place? The sun was up and the waves had died down to steady eight to ten foot swells lifting me up, then down, sickening. I threw up all over my shoulder, the retching stinging my throat and causing a painful rawness. I vomited all the salt water I had swallowed upon landing.

I looked around in the brightening dawn. The heavy mist and clouds had been swept away. The sky turned a bluish white, like the water inside the lagoon in Guam. The ocean was a slate gray with streaks of green and white foam. The force of the typhoon had passed.

I had to hold on, maybe someone would come. I vomited constantly, seasick beyond any flu I'd ever experienced. There was nothing left in my stomach and I could not stop retching. Could I survive this day? And another night? Surely, someone would be looking for us before long, surely those idiots at SAC Headquarters wouldn't keep playing games with our lives. Surely, this emergency would cause them to break radio silence, and tell someone we had crashed and there might be survivors. Surely, someone could save me.

For the first time in my life I was truly lonely. I thought back to all my friends I'd grown up with and about my buddies in pilot training. I made a deal with God that if he got me out of this mess, I'd preach His word for the rest of my life. And in the same breath, I cursed Him for doing this to me. I wanted to live. I had good reasons for living. I was just getting started in my Air Force career, hell, I'd only just made first lieutenant and was beginning to contribute my education and training to the Air Force. You can't do this to me! Damn it! I struggled to get through college and into pilot training, I worked hard! You just can't do this to me!

An hour went by. I was freezing in the sea and the wind. The waves washed over the raft, soaking me. The wind howled through the thin cotton material of my flight suit, sending shivers through my body. I didn't even know my location on this planet within a hundred miles.

My wristwatch was filled with water, but it continued to run. When the time for our Time-Over-Target arrived, I tried to stand up in the life raft and cheer toward Vietnam. I knelt in the raft and yelled encouragement to the guys dropping bombs on those bastard Viet Cong for killing civilians and Americans and otherwise brutalizing everybody around them.

Another hour passed. Far to the south a small dot grew on the horizon. What was it? A plane! There! Way to the south, there it was, a plane! I couldn't see what kind of plane it was but the speck grew larger. And then it turned away to the southwest and disappeared. Oh, the loneliness. It is impossible to measure loneliness in a tiny raft all alone in the sea.

Seasick! Ohhhh. It didn't stop. I barfed my guts out and then did it again and again. All the water I'd swallowed after hitting the waves had come up and left my mouth tasting like so much bile. It was in my throat and mouth, acid, burning salt in the wound. I couldn't stop throwing up. Waves, up and down, and up and down. The waves sucked the energy from my body, dehydrating me severely, sickening me, and just tossing me around like a dog playing with a toy.

I began to feel puny. I began to see how insignificant I was in this world, how small. My ego had been pumped up with all my schooling and training, and finally, flying with a great crew, some of the finest guys ever, my life dream come true, and now I was seeing the world in a new and entirely different manner. And probably I was going to die.

But somehow, while feeling like a speck of nothing, I also felt special. I felt very close to my God during the ordeal and, although I've since lost religion as a practice, I still felt at the time that maybe He was saving me for something, what I did not know.

What was that? A soft sort of whispering whine. I turned and met a KC-135 tanker almost face-on! The roar of its jets as it passed over me was as thrilling as it was startling. He pulled up a bit and started to circle me! He saw me! He's circling! I waved, I screamed at the top of my lungs, I waved. I was saved!

The tanker rolled out and flew away. But for only a few seconds. It did a teardrop turn and came back! He's turning to come over me again! He's diving on me. Oh, God, he's only fifty or a hundred feet off the water and, what's that? Above the left wing, the cargo door is open. Someone is standing in the door. He threw something out. Wow! A huge, 20-man, round life raft! If I can get to it, there will be water. And it's large enough that someone will see me. "I'm saved!" I yelled into the dying wind. "I'm saved!"

The large life raft dropped the short distance to the waves, inflating and wobbling like a falling rubber leaf. I skidded down into a trough, temporarily lost sight of the raft, bobbed back up to the top of another wave and—it was gone!

How could that be? I held my eyes on the spot and came up again to the top of the next swell, monotonously. The large raft and I were out of sync on the waves. It had fallen only yards from me but was gone! Oh, what a cruel trick. What a damned cruel trick! The tanker climbed higher, circled, and flew away. The loneliness got lonelier.

In total despair, I thought some of my crew might have died, and it all seemed unreal, like the crash hadn't happened. The other guys had just gone to another place, where I'd see them later. We'd meet in the club for dinner. How did heaven and hell come into existence? If there was an afterlife, would I see the others there? Would we someday drink a beer together again, maybe today? A great toast in the sky? Would I soon join them? Did any of them get blown to bits in the plane? What would it be like to die that way? Quick? What is it going to be like dying here in the sea?

Chapter Ten

For a social animal, loneliness is difficult to accept. I did not like it and accepted it badly. Oh, our dreams and fantasies gone astray, gone with the typhoon winds. The world is cruel and I'd been cloistered, and now I was to die a lonely death, halfway around the world from the ones I loved.

The sun was hot. I was cold. The sea was constant. Any time they wished, the devils of the sea could swallow me deep where I'd see the darkness close in and slowly lose my breath until I gasped uncontrollably and sucked in a lung full of water. It nearly happened! Then it would be quick—terrible but quick. My lungs would fill with salty seawater, and I guessed that a blackness would overtake me.

The waves calmed to about six feet from trough to crest and the wind died down to a gentle breeze. It was almost peaceful. Was it my imagination that the waves were so much higher, the wind so strong? Was it my imagination that I improbably saw two ships almost collide? How could I estimate the height of these waves? How strong was the wind when I landed? How could I estimate time when microseconds expanded into minutes? How could I be sure of anything? My world was so changed, I wondered if it was all a nightmare, or was I dead?

I sat and waited. For the first time in my memory I was absolutely, totally dependent upon someone else for help. There was nothing I could do but wait. If someone didn't save me, I'd soon die the horrible death of the deep, drowning in a foul-tasting brine that mixed with the bile in my gut. I threw up again. It hurt. It hurt worse than the time I got drunk in college and didn't know any better. The bile and salt water scraped against my throat, making it even more raw. If I swallowed any more water I'd have to throw it up again, always on my shoulder. I didn't care, the next wave washed it off anyway.

The sea was not at all like the beautiful lagoon at Tarague Beach. It was terrible, treacherous, full of devils, and as unforgiving of a mistake as flying in the air. Floating alone in the sea is completely frightening, flying alone in the sky is completely exhilarating. There is a loneliness to both that contains the same emotion but the feelings are at opposite poles. The difference is subtle. Flying is like floating gently on the ripples inside the reef where the pretty shells and prettier fish create a beauty of nature. Beyond the reef, the savagery of the open sea is like the nightmare of those few moments of terror when flying—it's like the terror of a plane crash.

Was that a shark fin? I saw a shark fin! Oh, Christ, I'm certain that was a shark, or am I dreaming again? Maybe the high waves kept the sharks down below and now that it is calmer the sharks are surfacing. Oh, Sweet Jesus! SHARKS! Will they attack me here in this little raft? Will they scrape the sides of the raft until it pops and then eat me like a pea from a pod? Dear God, that's a horrible way to die! I vomited again, my guts frothing through my throat into my foul-tasting mouth and I spit it onto my shoulder. Dear God, please don't let me get eaten in a shark frenzy.

How does a shark attack? What does he do? I lost the survival kit with shark repellent, unless they substituted seal repellent into my "Arctic Survival Kit." They say the repellent only hides you from the shark so he cannot see you in order to take a bite. But he can still smell my vomit and the blood from my cut fingers. Will he circle and get closer and closer until he makes his run to attack and chew me into bite-sized chunks? Will he think the raft is tasty and try to take a bite out of it?

I have the .38 military special revolver. I can shoot him. But if there are more than one . . . I'll save the last bullet for myself. Where is the best place to shoot myself? I really had to think of this stuff. God, if I ever live through this there will never be another thought in my head about suicide for the rest of my life. I want to live! But, where do I put a bullet into my brain for the best results, an instant kill? If I had to die and my choice was this, being eaten alive by these sea devils or shooting myself and giving up 30 seconds of life, then what would it be? It will be better once the sharks come in for their kill. Both ways will be quick but I'd rather not be conscious when the sharks take my arms and legs and then go after my face! Behind the right ear, that's where I'll shoot. One bullet, up into my brain and it will knock me out and into the sea and they will go into their frenzy.

That was a shark! I saw the fin! But now where did the son of a bitch go? Was he now waiting beneath the raft for me to just give up? Did he have friends who might want to share a fine meal of a young copilot? "Well screw you, shark!" I yelled. Severe depression then overcame me and I sat back in the raft and tried to force all thoughts from my troubled mind.

I'd made my peace with God. Or was it a bargain? I'd promised Him that if he saved my sweet ass, I'd preach His word for the rest of my natural life. I'd laid out all my chips. Now it was up to Him. What a dirty trick you pulled on me and my friends, God. What a nasty thing to do to someone who only wanted to explore space as an astronaut someday. Why did you let me get into this mess anyway? Damn it! Why are You doing this to me?

I found that dying was simple. I was going to die now and I knew it and accepted it with peaceful resignation. It would be quick, unlike the lingering pain of cancer or emphysema. God was playing a game of cat and mouse with me and I did not want to play the game any longer, I had a gun! I took out the gun and opened the revolver barrel. Six brass shells lay in the chambers and I removed one. The copper bullet fit tight into the brass casing and it was dry. Already the gun was rusting even though it had been oiled and well taken care of. The sea could do that, its nature was severe. I still have that bullet, as a reminder, in my jewelry box.

Death is a funny thing, inevitable, it happens. We fight it for as long as we can, accepting incredible hardships and torture until it finally envelops us. Sometimes death is quick and sometimes it is slow. How did the other guys die? I was certain some of them had to die in the crash or in their parachutes or in the sea. The thought passed through my mind that I would be the one to make the choice of who would die today and then, who would I choose? I didn't even know who the other crew was on the other B-52. If I were God, which of my crew would I want to live? And which other crew would I want that crashed into us? Would I be on any of their lists? It was a completely disgusting, horrible thought, and I tried to put it out of my mind and could not until I shouted into the sky at the top of my lungs, "I'M NOT GOD! Quit . . . tormenting . . . me . . . please."

I waited. The peaceful feeling grew stronger, the resignation to death accepted. I stopped shaking and shivering and was no longer cold. I no longer felt lonely. My muscles stopped hurting and I relaxed. I laid my arms over the side of the raft and let my legs hang over the end and

I floated, tempting the sharks below. The raft was a very bright yellow, colorful like the fish in the lagoon. It contrasted nicely with the white-blue sky and the now lighter, almost greenish-blue sea. The waves flattened more and no longer seemed threatening, wanting to flip me over and swallow me. Away from the raft, the sea itself was changing to a much lighter blue, peaceful and almost merging with the sky. The sun was brighter now and the wind was down to a gentle breeze, like at Tarague Beach. It almost seemed warm. I was at peace.

Had I accepted death? Was this the way it is before you die? Did my life flash before my eyes over the past four hours like the time warp of microseconds in the crash? I dreamed, allowing the waves to wash over me, and I laid back and closed my eyes. I no longer had to struggle. It just didn't matter anymore. If I was to die, there seemed no sense in fighting it any longer. I didn't want to die and I would struggle to my very last breath—but I was calm, resting, resigned to my fate, and in a very strange way, I was happy.

I lay in the raft like that for some undetermined time, dreamy, relaxed, unhurried with what little life I had left. The sun came through the clouds and warmed me and I stopped vomiting. In a weird way, I thought I finally had control over my life. If the sharks closed in, well then, I always had the gun. But even that seemed unnecessary. I waited, no longer lonely or alone. In my head I lay on the beach at Tarague and enjoyed my life. It was wonderful and quite peaceful. The monotony of the waves became soothing, rhythmic, peaceful, romantic, narcotic. I floated upward, hung for some undetermined length of time, and floated back down, down into the wetness, the womb. I floated back to my beginnings, before birth, before generations or even centuries, or eons. I was about to become part of the primordial soup. Soon I would become the food of some fish, excreted, and then food for something farther down the chain and deeper in the sea until finally, I would be mud on the bottom of the South China Sea. Parts of me might be carried into the Pacific Ocean, some bits into the Indian Ocean. In a twinkling, I would again be a molecular part of the universe, broken down into my elements and scattered to the seas, to the winds, to the world.

Someone once said you could scoop a cup of water from the sea, color it, and pour it back into the ocean and wait. Before long, in the archeological sense, after the waves have spread the cup of water evenly throughout the earth, you could take the same cup and scoop it full again from anywhere in the world. In that cup would be a few of the colored molecules from your original cup floating right there before your eyes. In a year, a hundred, I would again be part of the world. At that moment I became an agnostic, sort of to test it out—and it lasted until I was rescued. But was I still a child of God? I was no longer certain.

The mission and the other guys now seemed like a dream. Would they always be a dream, or would I see them again in this life back at the club or at the beach? Or must I wait until another life? Or see them in purgatory or heaven or hell? I did not know!

My water-filled watch still worked. It was almost eleven o'clock in Guam. The other B-52's would be far to the south of me now, returning to base. I could not have seen the contrails through the mist and clouds but the sky was a deeper blue, almost like the sky over Guam. I lay on the beach and closed my eyes and shivered a bit like when I was a kid and climbed out of a cold mountain stream to lie on a rock in the warm sun. But I was still cold! Shivers shook my body again with a force that hurt. My muscles cramped and my neck burned like hell itself. The calf of my left leg was in a lot of pain and my eyes stung with a fire like sulfuric acid had been poured into them, just for the torture.

What was that? It sounded like a gurgling bathtub drain! Was the sea about to swallow me? Was this the end coming? Was the sea now going to suck me down into its sewer? Was this how the monster of the deep was going to come and pull me under and eat me? Oh well, it just didn't matter. I laid back and rested my helmeted head against the back of the raft, my butt at the far end. How did a large man fit into this thing? I was 120 pounds and short and I barely fit. This raft was only an afterthought of Arctic survival planning.

There it was again! That gurgling sound. It floated on the breeze as I floated on the waves. It seemed to come from the southwest. I could hear it clearly when I topped the swells. I sat up. Nothing out there. Oh well. I laid back—but there it was again! Rhythmic, gurgling, almost mechanical. Was it a ship somewhere, far off like a mirage? I sat up again and stared far into the distance and . . . THERE IT WAS! A PLANE FLOATING ON THE SEA!

It bounced up and down on the waves, first its nose rising into the air and then its tail. Sometimes it spluttered, or sounded that way, across the waves as it dove into a swell and came popping back up and then down again.

Oh God, this is another dirty trick! What a sleazy way to torture someone, to let them die with the glimmer of hope fading into another hallucination. What hell, this torture, to let me hope and then hallucinate. And then to let me see this mirage that will fade into the slate-green sea, below the tops where small whitecaps still break and flay into froth and fling themselves against my face.

I unholstered my pistol, remembering the sharks and my decision. The seaplane dove and bounced in the waves, up and down, up and down, like I was doing. It got closer, and I could see it was a darker gray than the sea. It had two propeller engines high on the wings to keep them out of the water and it had two little floats that dropped to the water from near the wing tips. Below a small radar bulb on the nose, the keel broke to either side in scoops like the prow of a ship. The cockpit had windows, there were people in there! It was real! I might be saved!

"Hey! Hey, you guys! I'm here! Can't you see me?" I tried to stand up and could not. I tipped the barrel of my pistol down to empty the water out of it and then turned my head and held it up at arm's length and fired off three quick shots. They'll hear that! "Hey! Hey, can you guys see me?"

The waves seemed to calm down and the sea seemed to smooth and I felt I might have a future, that my life might go on. The feeling was like no other, before or since.

This seaplane looked exactly like every other seaplane I'd ever seen, even in the movies. Or was this the standard kind? I didn't care as long as it wasn't a dream. It taxied toward me! It was for real!

Directly in front of me, it was huge now, and it turned to its right and I could see people standing and waving to me from a door near the tail. I waved back at them.

Alongside me it turned right again. Then it reversed its propellers in order to back up to me. "Hey wait! That propeller is big and it's getting real close! Stop! Hey, you're going to slice me up with that prop!"

Screw this! There was no way I was going to let them chop me into little pieces after surviving this long and getting so close to rescue. The float near the left wing tip had a tie-down half-ring on it and it was only a couple of feet from my raft. I grabbed for it. Got it! I held on to it for life itself and there was nothing in this whole world that was going to get me to let go of that float! No 3,000-pound gorilla was strong enough, no beautiful, naked siren, even the Lorelei herself would never get me to release my hold on that float! General Curtis E. LeMay himself could come out here and order me to let go and I was not going to let go! If I released my grip, the bastards would chop me into bait. No way! I held on tight.

Neptune popped out of the water beside me! Now what was he doing in the South China Sea? He was a good-looking kid, much younger than I thought Neptune to be. He didn't have a long white beard or a trident. Who was this guy? What the hell was he doing in the middle of the South China Sea?

"Lieutenant, hey, let go. It's okay," he said. He actually spoke English. "Let go of the float." He had a crewcut and a wide smile and he was big. I thought he was going to laugh or tell a joke but he seemed to know I was serious. If he stayed around here for very long didn't he know he'd get chopped into bait too?

I glanced around and the propellers seemed to be in neutral, the pilot wasn't reversing them anymore so maybe they didn't intend to make fish bait out of us. I let go of the float and Neptune quickly pulled me to the open rear door of the seaplane.

Someone grabbed me and I found myself standing on something solid. It rocked up and down, which was nauseating, but I could see I was inside an airplane and there were real people in here! Someone slit my life raft and threw it back into the sea.

"Wait, I wanted to save that thing, it's important."

"We don't want to rescue an empty life raft again," said Neptune. He was right.

Somebody was wrapped in a blanket and strapped into

a seat. He looked like he'd been dragged through hell itself. Who was it? I recognized him, hey, it was Lieutenant Colonel Chuck Andermann!

"How are you? How you feelin'?" He looked positively white. God, he was a ghost. Did I look like that? Jesus, he looked bad.

"Ghahkloop ahhurp blahflaeynek," he said.

"What?" I yelled over the noise of the engines. He said something that sounded about like his first statement and I shouted, "Whose crew you on?" I couldn't remember every crew member and every AC. I wanted to know who we crashed into.

"Jahrhub seckhar, arbh kahak." He pointed toward the cockpit and indicated that the pilot of his crew was up front.

I could not only not hear him, I couldn't understand him. Every time he tried to talk he retched into a cut-in-half Mae West. Neptune and another ParaJumper (a PJ) stripped me down and wrapped me into a warm blanket. I was still freezing.

"He said, Joe Robertson," Neptune shouted into my ear. "Captain Robertson, he's up front."

I gazed forward and there, sitting in the jump seat, was Captain Joe Robertson, Aircraft Commander of one of our B-52's. I stared back at Colonel Andermann, who looked like death itself, and thought, "How in hell can Joe Robertson be in such good shape after this ordeal to help spot for survivors?" I knew Jim Marshall was Joe's copilot and I wondered if he was okay. I certainly hoped so.

The PJ's strapped me into a seat beside a porthole where I could see the left wing. On the other side was another porthole where I could see the right engine and propeller. Neptune cut one of my Mae Wests in half and said, "You can barf into this." I huddled and shivered and vomited and thought how happy I was.

The little porthole was my television to the world. All I had to do now was live and watch the sea. Others would take care of me. We taxied around and, within minutes, I spotted another guy in a life raft.

"Hey," I hollered at Neptune, "Hey, there's another guy!" I was elated and Neptune only nodded his head and bent over to look out my porthole. He probably thought he'd have to jump into the sea again to pull this one off the float too.

I wondered who the guy in the raft was. I hoped he was someone from my crew and thought back to Solomon's terrible choice that I had grappled with alone in my raft. We got closer and I could see it was Jim Erbes, our EW! He had survived! Oh man, if only we could pick up everyone.

Jim was bundled into the cabin with us and tied down, like me, across the aisle. I wanted to get up and run over and hug him but I figured I'd just get in the way. I hollered at him and waved and grinned and laughed. He did the same to me.

A few minutes later I saw another raft with someone waving from it. Wow! If we picked up people this fast we might soon get them all. Wouldn't that be great? Wouldn't that be fantastic? We could all go back to the club and have a beer and tell each other wild stories.

They pulled the other man into the plane and it was Jay Collier, our new navigator! Super! Oh, man, I'm so glad they got Jay, I like him so much. Now we're going to get everyone! Next we'll get Terry and the gunner and then Jim Gehrig. Wow! Soon we'll have the whole crew and then we can pick up Joe's crew! How could he be feeling so good as to be helping spot for survivors up in the cockpit? Survivors! We're all survivors! I was so glad to be a member of this kind of team where halfway around the world we can crash and in a few hours we get rescued by some of our own Air Force people. Man, oh man, we're all going to live. It's so great to be an American.

I looked at Neptune. He was a PJ. PJ's were the Air Force's equivalent of the Navy's SEALS and the Army's Special Forces except they had a corollary to their mission, rescue and extensive medical training for saving lives. Neptune was stoic, professional, and completely unmoved by extraordinary events.

We taxied around for a while, bobbing in the waves, but we didn't see any more life rafts. I began to worry that maybe we'd have to taxi to another area of the sea to find another group of survivors, or maybe a different seaplane had rescued them already.

On the floor of the cabin, in the middle of the aisle, was a round, red, metal plate. Water gushed from it like from an overflowing well. A lot of water. A young captain walked back to talk to us and he asked our names several times and copied down our service numbers. His name was Dave Haines, the copilot of the seaplane. I pointed to the bilge cover and he said that the bilge was full of water and we'd have to take off pretty soon or we'd sink!

Now, wait just a minute! We'd sink? You mean we'd be back in that devil ocean again if we didn't take off soon? He said that was correct. When they "landed" in the water it was really a crash into the waves and it cracked the hull. Oh, damn! We're going to die after all. And you guys threw away my raft!

I wanted to get down on my hands and knees and pound that bilge cover back into place and keep the sea out. I didn't ever want to go into the water again. For years afterward, I would take showers instead of baths and it would be decades before I ever waded again into the water at any public beach. I never again went to Tarague Beach.

Dave went forward and Neptune strapped himself onto a round, steel seat across the aisle and a bit forward from me. He was completely impassive.

And then the engines revved and we turned and started to take off into the wind over the swells. The engines were full power and I shivered in happiness as we accelerated. The seaplane bounced a couple of times and then we hit a wave, hard! I mean real hard. Then another. This was worse than our B-52 takeoff with bombs at full weight. We smacked into another wave even harder and the pilots worked her up onto the step, like when a motorboat gets its tail up and nose down and starts to really move. Except we hit the waves with a force that would tear apart any airplane I'd ever heard of.

The speed increased and we really got going, almost airborne now, it's getting easier, but only a little . . . and the engines quit! Now what? I looked at Neptune and he was still impassive. It didn't bother him. He knew all about this plane and what it could take. But Dave said we were sinking. Well, if it didn't bother Neptune then I wouldn't let it bother me. Right!

We took off again, same direction. Same waves, same pounding, and I wondered again if we'd break apart before we got into the air. Neptune sat there, stoic, looking at the floorboards, unconcerned. The red bilge cover started to gush again and he didn't even look at it! He wasn't worried. I was worried! In the past few hours, I had learned just how precious life is. I didn't want to die now after going through all this. Lord, you wouldn't let me die now after all this, would you?

We stopped again and tried to take off again. On the sixth or seventh try, I just knew we were going to die and sink into the primordial muck. We bounced along and the engines whined and got noisier and the waves hit the propellers and threw water forcefully against the side of the plane like in a hard hailstorm and we got up onto the step again and we bounced into the air.

The plane held for a moment, then fell onto another wave and bounced again, this time a little bit higher. Again onto the waves and again into the air. Up, come on, just a bit more. WHAM! WHAM! We hit the waves harder each time we bounced and we got a little higher each time. And then—we didn't bounce, we stayed . . . airborne! WE WERE AAAIRBOOORNE!

The plane struggled as it dumped the bilge water overboard and got lighter with each passing second. Every second was that much closer to home.

An engine must have coughed—or something. Suddenly, we banked steeply and fell and hit the water in a tremendous crash! It was even worse than the midair collision.

Everything spun around and then there was silence. I heard the low hum of an engine and the gentle slapping of the waves against the fuselage. Christ, we had crashed again! Were we going to sink right away now? I looked out my porthole and the left propeller sort of drifted around on its spindle but the right propeller was twisted and tied into knots. The bilge was gushing water steadily.

Jesus, sweet Jesus save us, we crashed again! There wasn't a blade on the right prop that was even worth junk. What did it do to the hull? It had to have broken with the force of the crash. We were probably going to sink right here very soon. Now what? Everyone was in deep trouble now, even the rescue crew.

Chapter Eleven

We gradually absorbed the fact that we had crashed. Again! That's twice in one day! Three airplanes! This had never happened before. I stared at the others. Dread showed clearly on Colonel Andermann's white face. In World War II, he'd suffered being shot down in a B-17 over Austria and was captured and held in Stalag Luft III where the POW's made the "Great Escape." He certainly didn't want to go back into the sea any more than I did.

Jim Erbes was a quiet person and he appeared calm but I could see he was worried. Jay was as worried as me, we caught it from the looks on each other's faces. Alarm registered behind our eyes, which were black dots surrounded by red where the white was supposed to be. I had to assume my eyes looked like his. We stared blankly at each other for a few seconds, and then I saw the red bilge cover floating down the aisle.

Obviously we were going to sink and we'd be in the water again, only this time without our life rafts. The PJ's had punctured and discarded all the rafts. "Sweet Mother of Mercy," I thought to myself—and I wasn't even Catholic. I hoped they had something on this plane we could use for a float.

I leaned over and looked forward into the cockpit. Ol' Joe Robertson was still hanging in there, a real trooper. I couldn't understand how he was able to do it. The rest of us were pretty banged up. My left calf was stiff and full of pain, as was my neck which, though I did not know it at the time, was "knocked off line" and all but broken.

Neptune jumped up and went forward. A half-minute later he came back and pointed out the porthole. "Look," he said. I raised up my sore body and looked out the porthole. Everything that had happened to me that day had been either a nightmare or a surreal dream. Strange things were coming back to haunt me and I was sure I'd wake up in bed to find myself sweating but now I wasn't certain about anything. About a quarter mile away, off our port side, as big and stable and as beautiful as any ship had ever appeared, was the black and orange vessel I'd seen in the eerie light before dawn—the ship that had nearly been rammed by the White Princess! My mind flashed back and forth between hallucination and reality and I was not certain that I was not now crazy. But that black and orange ship was real!

Within a minute, Neptune bundled us out of our seats and toward the back door. I was barely able to walk on my left leg, which hurt like hell. I held on to a railing beside the back door as a very narrow longboat glided up to it. The longboat was hardly more than a canoe and it certainly did not look seaworthy to me. The sailors in it motioned for us to climb aboard. Neptune and the other PJ gently helped Colonel Andermann because he had broken some ribs and was in severe pain. Jay, Jim, and I were basically ambulatory.

"What about my flight suit?" I asked, "and my helmet? I want my stuff, I'm nearly naked."

"It's okay, we'll bring it," said Neptune reassuringly.

Just before I stepped into the longboat I looked back up the aisle into the cockpit and asked Neptune, "Isn't Joe Robertson coming?"

He stared at me for a second with a strange look on his face and said, "No, Captain Robertson is dead."

I found myself standing in the longboat stunned. I couldn't speak. The pain of realization hit me with a tremendous force and I wanted to cry but again I had to fight the panic welling up inside my heart. For the first time I began to comprehend that some of the other guys were not going to be rescued. Ever! These were more than colleagues, these were my friends, my buddies, guys I'd worked with and lived with for nearly a year waiting for this Vietnam thing to begin. And some of them would not be going home.

The sailors in the longboat were Norwegian. The name on the prow of their orange and black ship was *Argo*. How interesting, the *Argo*. Wasn't Jason's ship the *Argo*? Was this something symbolic? Had I an adventure too? I'd just had one, and didn't yet realize that it would continue for years. Vietnam. Was it the beginning of another even greater adventure?

We came alongside the big ship and our tiny longboat/canoe banged into the side, rocking in the waves. A sailor threw a thick rope over the side of the *Argo* and one of the oarsmen helped me stand. He motioned for me to climb the rope to the deck about twenty feet above. Surely they had a rope ladder? I must have looked at him like he was crazy because there was no way I could make it up that rope in my condition. He motioned for me to climb the rope again. Both boats were crashing together and I remembered my Uncle Billy, who was aboard the battleship *West Virginia* during the attack on Pearl Harbor. He saw a man fall between the great, sinking battleship and a tender alongside. A wave rocked the two ships together and his words were unforgettable, "There was only a grease spot where the man fell and it washed away with the next wave."

The Norwegian sailor insisted I climb the rope so, rather than appear cowardly, I tried. I placed my feet against the side of the ship and walked upward until the rope was taut against the railing. I almost lost my grip, but my uncle's story goaded me on. A sailor reached over the side and pulled me across a wide, splintery wooden gunnel. Slivers embedded themselves into my naked side, and then, I stood on deck! I was alive! I was safe! WOW! I wanted to scream for joy. The great ordeal of fire, water, and air was over!

Lining the bridge railing, watching us in our elation and excitement, were two or three women and several children. I wore only wet, see-through jockey shorts and was basically naked and felt quite vulnerable.

I wondered how they would get Colonel Andermann up the rope with his broken ribs but the sailors tied it under his arms and hauled him carefully aboard. It must have been terribly painful. The sailors took him to their clinic and directed us through a door in the bridge structure that led to a large dining room with tables and benches.

A steward brought us trays of food and a sweet orange soda, motioning for us to eat and drink. We were grateful for their wonderful hospitality but we were all seasick. A sailor escorted us through another door into a bathroom which held the largest tub I've ever seen. It was about ten feet long and three feet wide. He indicated we should shower and he gave us each a robe to wear until they could wash and dry our flight suits.

I went first and luxuriated in the lukewarm freshwater spray. Jim and Jay quickly did the same, while I waited in the dining room and tried to drink a bit of soda. But my stomach disagreed with the attempt. The trays held small slices of delicious looking breads covered with lox, a fish pate, and tuna. Normally at a banquet I would have scarfed down as many goodies as possible, but today I had a slightly temperamental stomach. One look at a sardine and I wanted to throw up again.

The *Argo*'s captain visited us, and he spoke excellent English. He said a U.S. Navy ship had arrived alongside the ship to pick us up and take us to the Philippines. The Norwegian sailor brought our flight suits and he took special care handing me the Day-Glo orange survival knife that had saved my life. I opened it and showed him the switchblade and how the hook knife worked to cut the parachute lines. He displayed a great interest in the knife. So I gave it to him.

The captain escorted us to the railing, where a motor launch waited to take us to the USS *Point Defiance,* the Landing Ship Dock that had dropped the bathysphere, *Trieste,* to the bottom of the Marianas Trench off Guam, the deepest spot in the world's oceans. We boarded the launch by climbing down the same rope we had climbed up earlier. The launch rocked up and down in the waves and I wanted to throw up again. The seasickness would last for two days.

The *Point Defiance* dropped a moveable stairwell and, as we walked up to the deck, I turned to Jim and whispered, "What do we salute first? The flag or the officer of the deck?" Jim didn't know, or care, but I thought we were supposed to know these things in order to properly impress the Navy. I didn't see a flag or any formal officer, but a whole bunch of

Navy guys grabbed us and welcomed us aboard with hugs and handshakes.

They led us to the mess hall (ugh!). Philippine stewards brought us trays of good things to eat. I wanted to throw up again. We sat on round stools that swung out from under the table and we talked with everybody. The captain, a commander, entered and asked our names and serial numbers again. He sent a junior officer to report us survivors once again to somebody. Everyone seemed very concerned over exactly who was rescued and who was not. Then, with note pads and a tape recorder in hand, they asked us what had happened.

We then told our stories, for the first of several times. After a couple of weeks of telling the story, I would never want to talk of it again. I found out Jim Erbes was the one I'd seen in the parachute when mine had twisted and nearly collapsed on me. He was the one shooting flares and who'd nearly been run over by the *White Princess*. So, the *White Princess* was real after all! It made me feel a little less insane.

Later we heard that the KC-135 tanker that had dropped the twenty-man life raft to me had flown over the *Princess* trying to get her attention and to raise her officers on any frequency. But the *Princess* did not respond. Then the tanker pilot flew over the *Princess* at fifty feet and dumped jet fuel over her decks, trying once again to get her attention. But, nothing. The ship was a Japanese ocean liner on its way to Manila, and we would later learn that the captain lost his license for ignoring an international distress emergency. Captain Eric Hellberg, one of Mather's own drivers, was the pilot of the tanker. I owe him my life. In fact, I owe my life to quite a few people.

Jay's story was remarkable. After we had hit Joe Robertson's B-52, Terry had called out altitudes over the interphone, "Twenty-nine, twenty-eight, twenty-seven, twenty-six . . . " At twenty-five thousand feet he had turned to Jay and pointed his thumb down, indicating for him to eject. In a B-52 the navigators eject downward. Jay pulled the ring between his legs and ejected. He free-fell for a long time. When he thought his parachute should open, he waited some more, and then he pulled the D-ring. He stabilized, like a skydiver, and waited some more. But no chute!

Jay reached behind his back, intending to tear the nylon parachute out of its pack with his fingernails if necessary. That's when he found that he was still sitting in his ejection seat! He instinctively grasped for his lap-belt connector and almost released it. That would have killed him! He would have fallen to his death, still attached to a parachute that wouldn't open because it was connected to the ejection seat.

Jay had two handles on either side of his ejection seat, one to release the integrated harness and the other to release the seat survival kit from the parachute in order to stand up and manually bail out if necessary. He could not remember which handle was which. If he pulled the wrong handle, he would die. He was still falling from 25,000 feet! The Lady or the Tiger, with a twist—no time left in a free fall. He forced himself to, once again, read his B-52 flight manual, the *Dash One,* in his mind, and he concentrated on Chapter Three, Emergency Procedures. He read the chapter in his mind several times and could not find where it was written, which handle was which. It didn't work. He took his mind back to his B-52 training and went through three months of academics and flying and still, he could not remember!

The sea rushed up at him, and he tried another tack. To get out of the seat with the parachute attached but leaving the survival kit behind, you pull the right handle and then the left. He immediately jerked the left handle, watched his ejection seat hit the water as his parachute opened, and instantly, he was in the water! He had free-fallen 25,000 feet, only to have his parachute open within (as estimated later by the accident board) fifty feet of the sea! Now that's one helluva free fall!

I don't think he ever wants to try it again.

Colonel Chuck Andermann was the only survivor of Joe Robertson's crew from the other B-52. He said that when we had collided, their aircraft went into a spin, which was understandable since our right wing had sliced off their tail. The lateral g-forces threw him to one side like a child's doll. Try as he might, he could not get himself upright in his seat because of the spin-causing g's, and he thought of riding it all the way down. He had once bailed out of a burning B-17 and did not relish the thought of repeating the experience.

Chuck decided that it would be better to eject downward and take the chance that the downward g's would overcome the lateral spin g's and cause his head to be straightened. If he was wrong, his head would be left in the plane while his ejection seat fell along with his body into the sea. He really had no choice, so he pulled the ring between his legs and ejected, with his head over the side of the hatch. The force downward was just enough that he cleared the hatch. His parachute opened immediately and he floated down to the sea.

In the water, Chuck could not deploy his life raft and survival kit from its case and he spent quite a bit of time, with broken ribs, floating in the water and biting at the release cable with his teeth. The handle had broken off in the ejection. After breaking several teeth, he finally pulled the cable out and was able to crawl into his life raft.

While descending in his chute, Chuck had heard Joe Robertson screaming in pain. Joe, who'd also had no choice about ejecting with lateral g-forces, had ejected upward, with his arm out over the ejection armrest. Apparently, his arm was badly cut going through the hatch during his ejection. Joe was the first to be recovered by the seaplane guys, but he was found sitting in his life raft, dead from shock and loss of blood.

The captain of the *Point Defiance* said they were taking

us to Subic Bay in the Philippines. A battalion of Marines, the first to arrive in Vietnam with General Lew Walt when they had marched ashore at Da Nang, were aboard. They were returning to Hawaii after their combat tour and were a day ahead of the rest of their convoy. I would always feel bad about that, because they would end up losing two days taking us back to Subic Bay. Phillip Caputo, who wrote *A Rumor of War,* may have been aboard with us.

After we tried to eat a few spoonfuls of clear broth, the sailors took us to clean staterooms and showed us how to use the head and showers, and then we all took a nap. We had been awake for about 40 hours straight.

The *Point Defiance* had a large, deep bay that ran about half the length of the ship. In it were tanks and armored personnel carriers, still caked with the red mud of Vietnam. Some of the Marines were in the bay cleaning their equipment but they didn't seem to be in too big a hurry. They all had that "combat tour" stare, and they looked at us without saying much. Tony Muehling and Dave Haines, the seaplane pilots, finally came aboard. Tony was all excited and Dave was wild-eyed. As Tony told us what had happened, Dave emphasized everything with nods of enthusiasm.

It seems the Navy had got hold of Tony's sinking airplane and had sunk it. Tony had been attaching cables to the lift rings on top of the wings while Dave was in a raft underneath, securing things to hoist the seaplane aboard the ship. The Navy had done everything right but the plane was already wrecked. They hoisted it up toward the deck of the ship but, in the rolling waves, one wing slammed into the side of the ship. The plane spun, got caught on another wave, and its nose slammed into the side of the ship. It still wasn't over, though. The plane continued spinning and the other wing also got smashed, and when it did, the cables snapped and the plane fell right on Dave. But he dove down, barely escaping getting smacked and possibly lost at sea. His life raft was crushed.

Next they towed the plane to the rear of the ship where the LSD's doors could open and the plane could be pulled into the open bay beside the tanks and armored personnel carriers. Just as they were about to pull it in, the plane gave up. It tilted nose up, and slid under the water. That's three down so far! It made a great story, which I would hear at the Clark Officers' Club years later.

Tony was convinced the Air Force was going to court-martial him for losing his airplane. He was genuinely worried about it. Instead, he was decorated. Among other medals for this rescue, the American Legion awarded him their Valor Award in 1965 for his courage and ability in our rescue, at a large banquet in New York City. I hope it made him feel better.

The *Point Defiance* dropped anchor at Subic Bay. A motor launch took us ashore and, without delay, we were driven by bus around the bay to Cubi Point Naval Air Station and flown to Clark Air Force Base. We overflew the route of the infamous Bataan Death March of World War

II. We were ensconced in a hospital room marked "Top Se-cret," and we were not allowed to talk with anyone about the mission or the crash until the people from Guam ar-rived. So we all, especially Colonel Andermann, had a lot of fun teasing the nurses. The Colonel was quite the rake! He resembled Clark Gable and the nurses really went for him. They all flirted shamelessly. It was too bad he could not get out of bed. What was this thing about navigators, gunners, and fighter pilots? To all the ladies, we bomber pilots seemed to be invisible.

Colonel Fox, from Guam, arrived the next day to pick us up. We climbed aboard a C-97, the *Yokota Flyer,* for the trip back to Guam. We landed at dusk at Andersen and the entire squadron, including our maintenance people, was there to greet us. They had all spent a couple of solemn days waiting for us to return because we had all finally real-ized that eight of our men were gone. We were family, and now they were gone.

As we hobbled down the steps from the plane, Colo-nel Andermann first, we were mobbed. Colonel Parker grabbed my hand to shake it with enthusiasm, not realizing that I could barely walk, and I fell off the steps of the plane. Dave Roeder, a close friend and fellow copilot, caught me. Many years later, as an Air Attaché, Dave would be one of the 52 hostages held by Iran.

Colonel Parker took us to his quarters, plied us with Vat 69 scotch, which I could not drink, and had us tell our stories again. He wanted to hear, firsthand, what had happened, and he certainly had that right. I am, to this very day, convinced he would have become the commander of Strategic Air Command some years later had we not crashed. But the loss of two B-52's ended his progression, and he retired as a colonel a couple of years after our crash.

An accident board was in place the next day and we again told our stories—they were getting pretty stale to us by then. The President of the Accident Board was none other than three-star general Lieutenant General "Sundown" Wells, the Inspector General of the entire Air Force! He was nicknamed Sundown because, when he came on base, the commander there was usually fired and transferred by sundown that night! It had happened to General Ohlke. Also on the accident board were several other generals and a couple of full colonels. I had never, ever come face to face with a general in my whole career and for a young, brand-new first lieutenant it was heady stuff. I was scared stiff.

After a week we were allowed to go back to the States to recover from our wounds and to attend Joe Robertson's funeral and the memorial service for the others who were missing. The news of what had happened had been on television and had headlined on the front page of many newspapers, which people had saved for us. Every insurance salesman in Sacramento came to call on me about life insurance. I suppose we became oddities of a sort for a while.

I went to Georgine Gehrig's house one evening to tell that fine lady what had happened and how her husband had died. When I departed she gave me two sets of Jim's captain's bars, a cloth one for my flight suit jacket, which I would wear until I made major, and another set of pure silver bars for my "Class A" blues. At that moment, as I was leaving, it all released, and I broke down crying uncontrollably and inconsolably. In my heart I've been crying ever since.

The memorial service in the Mather Base Chapel overflowed with about two thousand people trying to attend. The next day Joe Robertson was buried in a local cemetery with full military honors. At the end of the service, when Taps was played, a B-52 flew over the cemetery low and very slow. We all cried unashamedly, as I do now, writing this.

I was granted two weeks leave to visit my family in Idaho, and Lieutenant General Ben LeBailey, from the Pentagon, who had grown up with my parents, came to ask me what had happened. He wanted to tell the story "firsthand" to his buddies at the Pentagon. After that, I didn't like telling the story, and have only related it a few times ever since. In fact, I disliked the story so much that it has taken thirty-seven years to write it. For me, it is unpleasant to even think about.

After we recovered, I flew another combat tour in B-52's with our "swim team" crew. We got a new AC, Major Pete Nichols, and a new gunner, Master Sergeant Charlie McCarthy. Major Bernie Dowes became our navigator when Jay got transferred and later we acquired Airman First Class Gary Class, almost a stutter, when Charlie retired. I'll bet Gary was glad to make Sergeant. On April 10, 1966, the last silver B-52F left Guam forever and, fittingly, our crew flew it home with Colonel Parker in the jump seat. He made the landing and, it seemed, the entire city of Sacramento was waiting for us. The camouflage "D's" took over in Guam and made history in Vietnam.

Just mention the words "Arc Light" to any Vietnam Veteran and watch the reaction on his face. Every single one of them will get a funny, awed look, remembering what those words meant to him and the power they held. Arc Light was the code name for B-52 operations throughout most of the war, and an Arc Light strike became one of the most impressive things to watch in the history of warfare.

After three years as a copilot, I had not moved up even one notch in crew ranking. I was still the "gofer" and I hardly got to touch the yoke in 1250 hours of flying the B-52, 360 of them in combat. I never got an aerial refueling. I, therefore, volunteered for anything in Vietnam, and got an F-105 assignment. After a seven-month check-out at Nellis Air Force Base in Las Vegas, I flew 156 missions in southeast Asia, 130 of them over North Vietnam. Countless of my friends were lost in the F-105; flying in one was considered one of the most dangerous jobs of the war. Only 100 missions were required for a ticket home, never to have to go back. But I kept going back for some reason, five combat tours total. It was many years before I realized I had a bad case of "survivor's guilt."

Later, I flew the F-111 and got exactly one percent of

all the combat missions flown in that plane during its era of combat. I flew only 30 combat missions in the F-111 because by then I was also a staff officer and had to work for my living. Staff guys did not get to fly too often. I discovered a cause for the "mysterious disappearances" of the F-111 and wrote some reports that got a "fix" on that outstanding airplane. We lost six F-111's and ten more good men during the Linebacker and Linebacker II Operations that ended the Vietnam War.

A few years ago I finally got up the courage to visit the Vietnam Veterans Memorial Wall in Washington, D.C. There, on the wall, are the names of 54 of my buddies lost during that conflict. The names of those killed start from the beginning of the war on the first slab and go to the right of the deep V of the wall, and it reads like a book from there. On the second panel to the right of the V, about chest level, are the names of those killed in our B-52 midair collision. If you are ever there, please touch their names, and say thanks for what they sacrificed for all of us.

James M. Gehrig, Jr.
Tyrrel G. Lowry
William E. Neville
Joe C. Robertson
James A. Marshall
Robert L. Armond
Frank P. Watson
Harold J. Roberts, Jr.